Taking Yourself Seriously

Processes of Research and Engagement

Peter J. Taylor & Jeremy Szteiter

The Pumping Station
Arlington, MA

© 2012 Peter J. Taylor and Jeremy Szteiter

Published by The Pumping Station
61 Cleveland Street #2, Arlington, MA 02474-6935, USA
thepumpingstation.org

Online purchasers of this book who have not paid sales tax in their own jurisdiction (bit.ly/SalesTaxRates) should file use tax returns to report the purchase.

Library of Congress Cataloging-in-Publication Data

Taking yourself seriously : processes of research and engagement / Peter J. Taylor, Jeremy Szteiter

   p. cm.

   Includes bibliographical references.

Library of Congress Control Number: 2011962371

ISBN 978-0-9849216-0-7 (pbk) 978-0-9849216-1-4 (cloth)

FIRST EDITION
Printed by Lightning Source in Gill Sans and Adobe Garamond Pro

Table of Contents

Acknowledgements

The most important thanks are to the many, many students in the research courses taught by Peter and, more recently, Jeremy who have allowed us to experiment with and refine the tools, processes, and frameworks presented in this book. Many people and several organizations have played a role at some point in the exploration and articulation of the tools, processes, and frameworks, and in their translation into book form. In chronological order—and with apologies to those whose contributions we have overlooked—thanks to Mac Post, Ann Blum, Greg Tewksbury, Peter Schwartz, Bruce Lewenstein, Mary K Redmond, Barbara Legendre, Keith Hjortshoj, Peter Elbow, Ken (Mac) Brown, Gwen Mills, Brenda Dervin, the International Society for Exploring Teaching Alternatives, the Institute of Cultural Affairs (Toronto), Duncan Holmes, Ellen Fogarty, Jo Nelson, Emmett Schaeffer, Tom Flanagan, the International Association of Facilitators, Steve Fifield, Allyn Bradford, Nina Greenwald, the New England Workshop on Science and Social Change, Vivette García-Deister, Mary Frangie, Kristen Bennett, Matthew Puma, Laura Rancatore, Cole Conlin, Jane LaChance, Michelle Hardy, Paul Dobbs, Chris Young, the Vision Studies Program at the University of Massachusetts Boston, Noah Rubin, Renessa Ciampa-Brewer, Michael Marcus, Paola Di Stefano, and Rebecca May. Finally, thanks to readers who submit suggestions for changes and additions to this book via the online forum, cctnetwork.ning.com/forum/topics/taking-yourself-seriously-a

OVERVIEW

Why another book on research and writing? The short answer: the approach presented here is not addressed well elsewhere. Most texts on research lay out the step-by-step decisions starting with identification of the problem. Or they review the theories and methods involved in various kinds of research. Texts on writing provide guidance and exercises to improve your writing skills. In contrast, this book presents frameworks and tools to help you become more *engaged* in research and writing.

Suppose you have a specific question or a general issue that seems worth investigating. Now reflect on your level of *engagement* with that research. Is it important to you personally? Does the inquiry really flow from your own aspirations (as against being directed to meet the expectations of others—advisors, funders, trendsetters in the field)? Will it help you take action to change your work, life, or wider social arrangements? Will it help you build relationships with others in such action, in pursuing the inquiry effectively, and in communicating the outcomes?

If you've answered yes in each instance, that is good to hear given that these questions are not emphasized in other research and writing texts. If you answered no or maybe not to any of the questions, consider this analogy. For a car engine to move the wheels, the gears need to be engaged with each other. Similarly, for your research and writing to move along well, you need to align your questions and ideas, your aspirations, your ability to take or influence action, and your relationships with other people. These concepts can be shortened to *head, heart, hands, and human connections*. The frameworks and tools in this book can help you bring these 4H's into alignment. That is what we mean by *engagement* and by inviting readers to take *yourself* seriously.

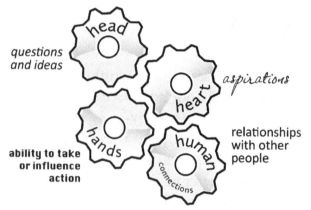

questions and ideas

aspirations

ability to take or influence action

relationships with other people

Engaging the "gears" of head, heart, hands, and human connections

One of us, Peter, has been teaching in interdisciplinary and non-traditional college programs since the mid 1980s. The approach presented in this book originated in a workshop-style research course in which his undergraduate students investigated issues about the social impact of science that concerned them, meaning they wanted to know more about it or advocate a change. The approach has been further developed through Peter's subsequent work in a mid-career personal and professional development graduate program where he has advised well over one hundred Master's students undertaking their final "synthesis" projects and has taught three research and writing courses that culminate in those synthesis projects. Students have brought to these courses very diverse interests and concerns—from demonstrating the routinisation of prenatal ultrasound screening to preparation for finding work as an editorial cartoonist; from adult education for low-income women to improving communication in the hospital operating room. (Jeremy was one of the mid-career Master's students; his interests at the time are illustrated in part 3.) Given the range of projects undertaken by students, the courses could not focus on specialized knowledge in any one discipline, nor could students expect the instructor to be an expert in all of their areas of interest. Addressing the challenge of supporting students with diverse projects to take themselves seriously has led to the development or refinement of many tools and processes. (Peter's pedagogical journey is captured in a series of snapshots that make up, Teaching and Learning for Reflective Practice, the first section of Part 4.) The five innovations to follow lie at the heart of what researchers or researchers-in-training will find assembled in this book.

Five innovations

1. A framework of ten phases of research and engagement that you move through, then revisit in light of two forms of feedback: responses by advisors and peers to the writing and oral reports you share with them; and what you learn using tools from the other phases. This sequence and iteration helps you as a researcher define projects in which you take your personal and professional aspirations seriously. (Doing so may mean letting go of preconceptions of what you *ought* to be doing.) These phases are presented in Part 1. Descriptions of the **tools and processes**, given in alphabetical order, make up Part 2. Part 3 includes illustrations of their use in the development of a project Jeremy undertook on engaging adult learning communities in using the principles of theater arts to prepare them to create social change.

2. A cycles and epicycles framework for Action Research that emphasizes *reflection and dialogue* through which you revisit and revise the ideas you have about what action is needed and about how to build a constituency to implement the change. Such reflection and dialogue adds "epicycles" to the traditional Action Research cycle (i.e., problem-> data-> action-> evaluate outcomes->next steps...). The cycles and epicycles framework is presented in overview in Part 1, which includes a list of tools useful for the reflection and dialogue, constituency building, evaluation and inquiry, and planning that contribute to Action Research. Descriptions of the tools are also included in Part 2. Part 3 includes excerpts from a second project of Jeremy's, involving collaborative play among teachers in curriculum planning, which illustrate the framework by conveying the experience of someone learning to use it.

3. Dialogue around written work: Written and spoken comments on each installment of a project and on successive revision in response to the comments. Dialogue creates the chance for you and your advisors (or instructors) to recognize and understand perspectives separate from your own, and then revisit your ideas by putting alternatives in tension with them. If your advisors assemble a portfolio of your installments and comments, they can look back over them when they interact with you. This makes it more likely —even when they are not an expert in your project's topic—that the unfolding dialogue helps you bring to the surface, form, and articulate your ideas as a researcher. Dialogue around written work is evident in the illustrations in Part 3 and discussed further in the snapshots on Teaching and Learning for Reflective Practice in Part 4. (You might choose to read that section first if, before jumping into the practical details, you want to have a view of Peter's development as a college teacher and the journey through which the tools and processes have emerged.)

4. Making space for taking initiative in and through relationships: Don't expect to learn or change without: negotiating power and standards (a "vertical" relationship); building peer (or "horizontal") relationships; exploring difference; acknowledging that affect is involved in what you're doing and not doing (and in how others respond to that); developing autonomy (so that you are neither too sensitive nor impervious to feedback); and clearing away distractions from other sources (present and past) so you can "be here now." These aspects of teaching-learning relationships do not always pull you in the same direction, so it is difficult to attend to all six aspects simultaneously. Instead, expect to *jostle* among them. (The idea that you keep many considerations in mind, but focus on a few at any given time informs the book's approach as a whole; see the discussion in Part 4 of Teaching and Learning for Reflective Practice.)

5. Creative habits for synthesis of theory and practice: A framework for that point in your life when you take up the challenge of writing something that synthesizes your theory and practice. Everyone has a voice that should be heard. The creative habits introduced in Part 1 and described in Part 2, together with the other frameworks and practices above, constitute a structure of support—including support from yourself—that enables you to find your voice, clarify and develop your thoughts, and express that voice in a completed written product.

How to use this book?

Like a field-book, it is something you might simply refer to from time to time, looking for tools and processes to adopt or adapt in your current endeavors. (For terms given in **Bold Face** or Capitalised readers can find details in the relevant section of Part 1, Phases, Cycles and Habits, or in the entries that make up Part 2, Tools and Processes.) We hope, however, that at some point you decide to move systematically through the Phases, Cycles, or Habits for Synthesis. These frameworks are structures intended to guide readers—whether you are a college student or a more experienced professional—as you develop as researchers, writers, and agents of change. (The frameworks also lend themselves to adaptation by teachers and advisors designing semester-length courses.)

Of course, the kind of help derived from the book depends on where in the spectrum of researcher or researcher-in-training you lie. Just as some children learn to read with little instruction, there are some students who have little trouble learning to define a hypothesis that can be studied with the methods of their discipline and are comfortable using the standard writing conventions and publication format to report on research. If you operate at that end of the spectrum, you may view the integration of the 4H's that emerges through the five frameworks and practices above as a way to help you branch out in new directions and to avoid simply continuing along previous lines. However, perhaps you are at the other end of the spectrum—you may feel alienated from the expectations of any one discipline and struggle to complete your research and writing assignments. If so, view this book as a way to keep your eye not on the supposed prize of the completed project, but on the possibility of developing a project that engages you. To find such a project you need to push the expectations of others aside for long enough to explore how to connect your head with your heart, to give voice to your aspirations, to build connections with others and to change your work, lives, and wider social arrangements.

Then again, perhaps you lie in between these two poles—you might be a diligent student or researcher who eventually meets disciplinary standards, but you ask for more input in generating research questions and editing written work than your advisors like and take longer than everyone had hoped. You may be susceptible to doubt and procrastination—am I really doing something worthwhile for society and for myself? If this picture fits, you might pay more attention to the 4H's as a way to become more confident and comfortable about the directions of research and engagement that you choose. Wherever you lie in the range of students and researchers, the variety of tools for research and writing presented here constitute an invitation to you to take yourself seriously.

There are, of course, many more research tools and processes than are included in this book. The Connections and Extensions that make up Part 4 provide some entry points for students and teachers to explore the insights, experiences, and information from a wider world of research, writing, and engagement in change. An Internet search of syllabi for research courses will yield texts that lay out the steps, decisions, and theories involved in research in any given field. This book cannot substitute for the knowledge, perspectives, and debates in specific fields. That said, our approach can serve as a valuable complement to specialized texts, providing a scaffolding for you to explore new directions of wholehearted engagement with others—and with yourself.

I
PHASES, CYCLES & HABITS

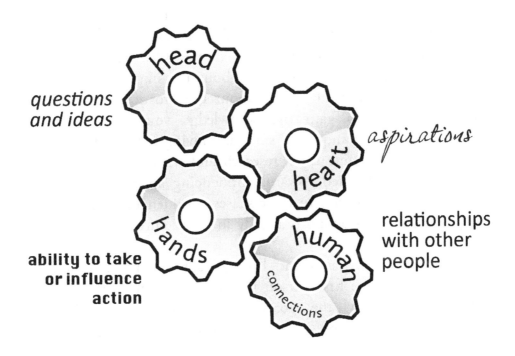

questions and ideas

aspirations

ability to take or influence action

relationships with other people

PHASES of RESEARCH and ENGAGEMENT

The Phases framework emphasizes research and writing that prepares you to communicate with an audience. The **Cycles and Epicycles of Action Research** constitute a complementary framework, emphasizing reflection and dialogue through which you build a constituency around some course of action. However, the distinction between the two kinds of research is not sharp. When following one of the frameworks, you may find yourself borrowing tools introduced under the other. You should feel free to develop your own synthesis of the two frameworks. After all, Action Research builds from knowledge about the impact of actions that others have already taken and about the broader background for those actions. To gain this knowledge you need a systematic approach for your inquiries, such as moving through the phases of research. At the same time, research and writing under the Phases framework is directed towards influencing an audience about an issue that engages you. In these senses—influencing others or being engaged yourself—action is already in the picture.

Each Phase of Research and Engagement is defined by a distinct goal, stated in the first person below. (The goals of the Phases are complemented by the goals of developing as a **Reflective Practitioner** that apply through the whole project.) Keep in mind, however, that the phases are *overlapping* and *iterative*. That is, allow yourself to revisit a phase later in light of the following:
• other people's responses to what you share with them; and
• what you learn in other phases (which may include seeing that you had not really met the goals of some earlier phases).

Later phases (especially, F and I) may be started early if opportunities arise during your particular project. In general, however, because each phase builds on the ones before, it is best to start them in the order given. Moving through the sequence of phases below and allowing for iterative development should help you reflect on any prior conceptions of what you thought you *ought* to be doing and home in on a research project in which you are taking your personal and professional aspirations seriously.

As indicated in the chart at the end, the tools and processes introduced under each phase are organized in relation to fourteen *sessions*, which could be weeks in a semester-long course or fractions of the total time available for the project.

A. Overall Vision
Goal: "I can convey who I want to influence or affect concerning what (Subject, Audience, Purpose)."

B. Background Information
Goal: "I know what others have done before, either in the form of writing or action, that informs and connects with my project, and I know what others are doing now."

C. Possible Directions and Priorities
Goal: "I have teased out my vision, so as to expand my view of issues associated with the project, expose possible new directions, clarify direction or scope within the larger set of issues, and decide the most important direction."

D. Component Propositions
Goal: "I have identified the premises and propositions that my project depends on, and can state counter-propositions. I have taken stock of the thinking and research I need to do to counter those counter-propositions or to revise my own propositions."

E. Design of Further Research and Engagement
Goal: "I have clear objectives with respect to product—both written and practice—and process—including my personal development as a reflective practitioner. I have arranged my work in a sequence (with realistic deadlines) to realize these objectives."

F. Direct Information, Models and Experience
Goal: "I have gained direct information, models, and experience not readily available from other sources."

G. Clarification through Communication

Goal: "I have clarified the overall progression or argument underlying my research and the written reports."

H. Compelling Communication

Goal: "My writing and other products grab the attention of the readers or audience, orient them, move them along in steps, so they appreciate the position I've led them to."

I. Engagement with Others

Goal: "I have facilitated new avenues of classroom, workplace, and public participation."

J. Taking Stock

Goal: "To feed into my future learning and other work, I have taken stock of what has been working well and what needs changing."

Suggested session (numbered) to begin to emphasize each phase (A-J) and to use selected tools and processes

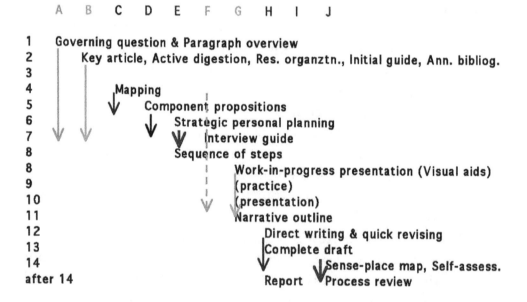

Suggested pacing for moving through the phases

Phase A—Overall Vision

Goal

"I can convey who I want to influence or affect concerning what (Subject, Audience, Purpose)."

Tools and Processes (introduced in this phase)

Governing Question and **Paragraph Overview** of project
Think-Pair-Share
Dialogue around Written Work
One-on-one Session
Freewriting
Models from the Past
Sharing of Written Work

Remember: For terms in **Bold Face** or Capitalised, you can find more detail in the separate entries of Part 2, Tools and Processes, unless the term refers to another Phase, in which case consult this series of entries.

Sequence

Remember: The tools and processes introduced under each phase are organized in relation to fourteen sessions. These could be weeks in a semester-long course or fractions of the total time available for the project.

In session 1
Think-Pair-Share on:
• your area of interest
• the specific case(s) you plan to consider
• the more general statement of the problem or issue beyond the specific case

- how you became concerned about this case or area
- what you want to know about this case or area by the end of the semester
- what action you think someone should be taking on this issue (specify who)
- what obstacles you foresee and what help you might need in doing the research
- who the audience for your research report might be

Initial formulation of **Governing Question** and **Paragraph Overview** for the proposed project. Do not expect to digest everything in the descriptions of Governing Question and Paragraph Overview right away. Over time you will develop a better idea of these tools by revising in response to comments, that is, through **Dialogue Around Written Work**. Indeed, the point is not to have your project defined at the very start and then to stick with that, but to begin an ongoing, iterative process of defining and refining the project. Eventually you can home in on a well-considered question and statement that guides your work and priorities as you move ahead and guides the feedback others give you on your work. A key part of homing in is making clear to yourself and readers the subject, audience and purpose of your project: Who you want to reach? What you want to convey to them? Why do *you* want to address them about that?

Sharing of Written Work: Read your question and paragraph to the group to hear how it sounds shared out loud with others.

After session 1
Freewriting: Try this out for ten minutes at least a few times a week. Perhaps it may become a valued **Creative Habit** that you continue throughout any project.

One-on-one Session: Discuss your ideas with an advisor (or instructor) in a scheduled face-to-face or phone meeting early on in the project—by session 5 at the latest.

Models from the Past: Review reports from related projects in the past to get a sense of their scope and the look of the final products.

Sharing of Written Work: Keep sharing your written work with peers. Indeed, sharing runs through the entire process of research and writing.

Begin **Phase B**. Finding out what others have done that connects with your proposed project usually leads you to refine your own sense of subject, audience, and purpose.

By session 3
In Dialogue around Written Work you get comments from your advisor and respond to them. Through this, you will generate revised versions of your Governing Question and Paragraph Overview of the project.

Follow-up

Iterative Development: Your topic will change or be more focused as time goes on, so, with each new Phase, take stock of that and start subsequent submissions and any work you share with the latest revision of your Governing Question and Paragraph Overview. Trying to write a tighter overview will also help to expose shifts, gaps, and ambiguities in your project. The Paragraph Overview may, after several revisions, find its way into the introduction of your report and the Governing Question may, somewhat shortened, be reflected in your report's title. Shifts, gaps, and ambiguities also get exposed and explored through Dialogue around Written Work, Sharing of Written Work, and One-on-one Sessions with advisors. These processes should continue throughout the Phases of Research and Engagement.

Begin **Phase J**, Taking Stock of your process, which includes progress towards the goals of the **Phases** as well as the goals of developing as a **Reflective Practitioner**. Continue taking stock throughout the project so as to feed back into your learning, into your learning about learning, and into your advisor's (instructor's) learning about how their advisees (students) learn.

Phase B—Background Information

Goal

"I know what others have done before, either in the form of writing or action, that informs and connects with my project, and I know what others are doing now."

Background

Once you have an initial formulation of your proposed project (**Phase A**), you can start to find out what others have done that informs and connects with that project. This research can influence your project in several ways: You can build on what others have written and done; you can make connections with others in your area and cultivate them as supporters of your work; you refine your project formulation after noticing what grabs you and what turns you off about what others have written and done; and you expand your view of what your project entails.

Tools and Processes

5 F's
Key Article
Initial Guide
Active Digestion of readings and conversations
Sense-Making Response
Annotation of Bibliography entries

Sequence

5 F's: All through your background research allow for a continuing interplay among Find, Focus, Filter, Face Fears, and File.

In session 2

Learn or refresh bibliographic searching skills using guides provided by your University or public library. Use databases to locate articles or sections in books that provide what you need to move forward in your research. In order to identify the range of publications relevant to your project now—rather than when it is too late in the project to be useful—look especially for a **Key Article** that provides you with a rich set of references to follow up on (and thus move you towards meeting the goal of Phase B).

After session 2

Establish an off-site connection to a University or public library, bookmarking the link on your internet browser. Establish your on-paper and on-computer **Research Organization**, which includes your bibliographic and note-taking systems, your **Personal and Professional Development (PPD) Workbook**, and filing of research materials and any other handouts.

Continue background library, Internet, and phone research to find out what others have written and done that informs your evolving project and who is doing what now. **Actively digest** what you read and conversations you have (using the **Five F's**, **Annotating your Bibliography** or spelling out a **Sense-Making Response**). Digestion is essential because, if your project is to progress, you have to sort out which of the many articles that you locate provide information that you need and to clarify how they connect with your project. Allow yourself to work on both the *creative* and the *critical* aspects—opening up your topic to more and more considerations, and seeking order and priority in the overabundance of material produced by the creative aspect. As Elbow (1981, p. 8-12) recommends, alternate these aspects, so as not to let one stifle the other, as you define and refine a manageable project.

If, at first, you do not find written material on your topic, do not give up. Even if what you are doing turns out to be unique, searching for the work of others will clarify the ways in which your topic is unique. It is a common trap to say you have tried and failed to find something when, actually, you are protecting yourself from unarticulated fears and self-doubts by not trying very hard, making time, asking for help, following leads, and so on. It is better to face your fears now rather than have them limit what you can do. In that spirit, identify an **Initial Guide** for your inquiries in their early unformed stage and arrange to talk with that person.

By session 3
For an article or section in a book you have found, submit a **sense-making** response to show how it affirms and extends your thinking about your proposed research.

By session 4
Have the following assignments ready for your advisor and peers to hear about or read: **Initial guide**, **Key article**, and initial version of your **Annotated bibliography**.

Follow-up

By session 4 the materials that you have located and digested may have led to a number of revisions of your **Governing Question**. You may also be overwhelmed by how much you are finding out, in which case you are ready to clarify direction through the activities of **Phase C**. Even as you move ahead, continue to locate and digest what others have written and done. You might well find yourself near the end of the time available for your project before you can say that you have met the goal of Phase B.

Phase C—Possible Directions and Priorities

Goal

"I have teased out my vision, so as to expand my view of issues associated with the project, expose possible new directions, clarify direction and scope within the larger set of issues, and decide the most important direction."

Background

After a couple of weeks learning about what others have written and done (**Phase B**), you probably have an expanded view of issues associated with your project. It may seem pressing to define a narrower topic. However, this phase works towards clarification of your direction by first *expanding* your view of the issues even further. (This matches Elbow's [1981] advice to alternate between creative and critical aspects of writing as well as "opening-wide, then focusing in & formulating," a process noted in Part 4's Teaching and Learning for Reflective Practice.)

Tools and Processes

Mapping
Questions for Opening Wide and Probing
Pyramid of Questions
Ten Questions
Sense-Making contextualization applied to your whole project

Sequence

In session 4
Create a draft version of your map, prepared with the help of the **Questions for Opening Wide and Probing**.

Work with a peer to review your map, using the same probing questions. Consider how the map relates to your **Governing Question**.

Supplementary processes for opening wide or focusing and formulating: **Pyramid Of Questions**; **Ten Questions**; **Sense-making** contextualization applied to one's whole project; and discussion with advisor and peers (see **Sharing of Work to Elicit Responses** and **One-on-one Session**).

By session 5
Revise your draft map, working with a peer to review it using the probing questions.
Compose a revised Governing Question.
Submit the map and revised Governing Question to your advisor for review.

Follow up

In **Phase D** you identify areas that require further research, but do so without the visual or graphic approach that is at the heart of Mapping. You might take note of the similarities and differences between what emerges in Phases C and D in relation to the interplay of the creative—opening wider—and critical—focusing in —aspects of your thinking. Like Mapping, Phase D comes *before* you can complete an overall **Research Design** or clarify your **Overall Argument**.

Phase D—Component Propositions

Goal

"I have identified the premises and propositions that my project depends on, and can state counter-propositions. I have taken stock of the thinking and research I need to do to counter those counter-propositions or to revise my own propositions."

Background

Suppose that you have started getting a handle on what others have written and done (**Phase B**) and have clarified the direction of your project (**Phase C**). Yet, you still find yourself focusing on work that supports your views while avoiding opposing views. Now is the time, then, to *tease out* the additional research needed to prepare yourself to address an audience that does not already share your views.

Tools and Processes

Component Propositions

Sequence

Note: The **Component Propositions** process opens your project even wider, but, without this, you run the risk of finding yourself, when time for new research is short, seeing that you needed to have paid more attention to alternatives to the propositions that underlie your project. You might take note of the similarities and differences between what emerges in Phases C and D in relation to the interplay of the creative—opening wider—and critical—focusing in—aspects of your thinking.

In session 5

Begin to use the **Component Propositions** process to take stock of the thinking (e.g., including revision of your propositions) and research that is needed in addition to the central strands of your project.

By session 6

For four to six different propositions, summarize the counter-propositions and counter-counter propositions, and identify any areas that need more research that have been exposed.

Follow up

Keep a list of the areas needing more research in front of you when you prepare your design for further research and engagement during **Phase E**.

Phase E—Design of Further Research and Engagement

Goal

"I have clear objectives with respect to product—both written and practice—and process—including my personal development as a reflective practitioner. I have arranged my work in a sequence (with realistic deadlines) to realize these objectives."

Background

You are probably around a third of your way into the time allotted for your project. Having identified many and varied research tasks to prepare you to write a compelling report (**Phase D**), you now need to prioritize those tasks and perhaps adjust how you are framing your project (**Phase A**). Phase E approaches the design of the research and engagement ahead by articulating a broader vision for your work that integrates your reflection on the **Reflective Practitioner Goals**. This broader vision should motivate and guide you in completing the tasks that you work into your design.

Tools and Processes

Strategic Personal Planning
Research and Engagement Design

Sequence

Note: The word *design* in phase E refers primarily to planning so that you can undertake what you really need to do during the course of completing your project. This planning is easier said than done. This sense of design does not encompass preparation of effective questionnaires, determining a statistically valid sample of people to complete them, and so on. As an entry point into that kind of research design, see suggestions in the Resources section of Part 4.

In session 6
Review the **Reflective Practitioner Goals**.
Strategic Personal Planning through the first stage: Practical Vision.

By session 7
Time permitting, complete the full **Strategic Personal Planning**, proceeding from Practical Vision through the three subsequent stages: Underlying Obstacles, Strategic Directions, and Action Plans. If pressed for time, you might use **Freewriting** to formulate Action Plans directly after the Practical Vision stage.

By session 8
Complete a **Research and Engagement Design** that lays out a realistic sequence of completable steps to realize your vision for the project and overcome anticipated obstacles.

Follow up

We all know what it is like to make plans or to-do lists that get eclipsed by other calls on our time and attention. If this starts to happen—or even before it has a chance to happen—arrange a buddy to check in with each day, if only to make sure that both of you have made time to review your practical vision, design, and specific action plans. Indeed, this is the appropriate point—if that has not happened already—for discussion with your peers about establishing a **Support and Coaching Structure** to get everyone to finish their research and writing in the time available.

Phase F—Direct Information, Models and Experience

Goal

"I have gained direct information, models, and experience not readily available from other sources."

Background

The opportunity to interview or observe someone whose work is central to your subject may arise at any time during your project. This phase is inserted at this point not to say you should refrain from interviewing until now, but because it usually takes you some time to find out what can be learned from other sources and to formulate the questions that can best be answered directly. In Phase F you aim to get access to the kinds of experiences that are not in the published literature or other available records. (If you want to get someone's suggestions of what to read, who to contact, or other guidance, think of that as talking with an **Initial Guide** for **Phase B**, not as interviewing.)

Tools and Processes

Interview Guide
Interviewing
Questionnaires and Surveys
Observation
Evaluation
Participant Observation

Sequence

By session 7
Write down five questions you would like someone to answer for

you—not just any questions, but ones for which you cannot easily get answers from published literature. For example, you might need help from practitioners or activists in interpreting the controversies and politics around your issue.

During session 7

Draft an **Interview Guide**. Write out fully your opening and closing script in your interview guide, but an outline is usually sufficient for what lies in-between.

Practice interviewing using the Interview Guide. Set the scene for a peer and ask them to ad lib responses that your interviewee might give.

Refine the Interview Guide based on this practice interview.

After session 7

If there is someone you can interview who would help you meet the goal of this phase, undertake the following: Establish contact with them and schedule interviews. Finalize the interview guide. Do mock interviews in which you practice using the release forms (see **Interview Guide** and recording equipment. Conduct interviews. Digest recordings or notes.

Refer to a conventional text on social science research methods, such as Schloss and Smith (1999) for more detail on the practice of interviewing and for guidance on the following items:

Questionnaires & Surveys

Conduct a pilot survey or questionnaire, revise it in light of how it went, then implement the revised version.

Observation

Identify practitioners who can demonstrate their work.
Attend demonstrations of practices that might be incorporated in project.

Evaluating

Prepare **Evaluations**, conduct them, and analyze the data.

Participant Observation

Arrange participant observation at workshops on practices that might be incorporated in project.

Follow up

After the interview, observation, etc.

Prepare a brief written report on interview conducted, participant observation, workshop experience, or evaluation. Write this report in a form that is useful to you in drafting your project report—do not address the report to your advisor. There is no need to give blow by blow or a full transcript. Focus instead on the "direct information, models, and experience [you gained] not readily available from other sources."

Phase G—Clarification through Communication

Goal

"I have clarified the overall progression or argument underlying my research and the written reports I am starting to prepare."

Background

Preparing to communicate about your project does not presuppose that you have finished your planned research. That could continue until the day you submit your final report. Indeed, at this half-way point in the project, you will probably still be refining the direction (Phase **A** and **C**) and scope (Phase **D** and **E**) of your research as well as filling in Background Information (**Phase B**). In Phase G, which spans several sessions, you clarify your thinking by preparing to communicate your work-in-progress to others, all the while continuing your research.

Tools and Processes

Overall Argument—Clarification
Work-in-Progress Presentation
Visual Aids
Narrative Outline
Writing Preferences

Sequence

In session 8
Extract the **Overall Argument** stated or implied in a previous researcher's project report.
Draft a sequence of **Visual Aids**, both to prepare for **Work-in-Progress Presentation** and to clarify your Overall Argument.

In session 9
Take a turn practicing your Work-in-Progress Presentation in front of a subset of your peers. From everyone's feedback to each other and from your own experience doing your practice run, clarify further your Overall Argument and revise your Visual Aids.

In session 10
Work-in-Progress Presentation to all your peers, advisors, and, if possible, a wider audience with feedback given in **Plus-Delta** mode or, time permitting, through more extended Q&A periods.

After session 10
Digest feedback on Work-in-Progress Presentation.
Building on your Work-in-Progress Presentation, start the process of outlining, writing, and revision, all the while continuing your research.

By session 11
Complete a **Narrative Outline**. Resist the temptation to give your report a short, cryptic title. Instead, create a long and descriptive title, because that helps to orient your readers as well as keeping you on track as you write. Follow the title by your **Governing Question** and **Paragraph Overview**, both of which may need to be revised since your most recent submission. Having all these items at the start of the outline will help you monitor whether you are writing what you set out to. It will also help readers offer well-focused feedback.

Around session 11
Explore your **Writing Preferences** to identify strengths you can rely on and skills you need to work hard to develop.

Follow up

As you draft and revise your writing under **Phase H**, Compelling Communication, continue to work on clarifying and refining your

Overall Argument and keep in mind what you have learned by exploring your **Writing Preferences**.

Phase H—Compelling Communication

Goal

"My writing and other products grab the attention of the readers or audience, orient them, move them along in steps, so they appreciate the position I've led them to."

Background

When you prepared your **Work-in-Progress Presentation**, you should have highlighted the key steps in getting your intended audience to appreciate the position you want to lead them to. Through feedback and fleshing out the presentation into a **Narrative Outline**, you have a firm basis for Phase H, in which you complete a draft report then revise it in response to feedback.

Tools and Processes

GOSP
Direct Writing and Quick Revising
Drafts (Narrative and Complete Draft, Final report)
Sharing of Work to Elicit Responses
Revising
Reverse Outlining

Sequence

Note: You should not expect to work out your ideas in one attempt—every writer needs to revise! **Revision** should be proactive, that is, do not wait for your advisors to slog their way through a rough draft and do the work for you of identifying problems in your exposition.

In session 12
Direct Writing and Quick Revising for 90 minutes with the goal of completing a narrative **Draft** (say 4-5 pages), which, as in the **Narrative Outline**, focuses on the explanatory sentences that indicate the point of each section (and subsection) and interconnections among sections. Then read section III of Elbow (1981) to get you into the mood for revising.

By session 13
Building on your Narrative Outline or Draft, and taking stock of comments received on them, prepare a complete **Draft** of your research report. For a Draft to be *complete* you have to get to the end, even if you only sketch some sections along the way. An incomplete Draft usually leaves readers (and yourself) unsure if you are clear about the position you want to lead them to and the steps needed to get them there.

In session 13
Sharing of Work to Elicit Responses: After the draft is completed, pair up with a peer and comment on each others' draft.
Reverse Outlining may be needed if a draft report does not **GOSP** readers well.

After session 13
Revise the complete **Draft** with a view to submit a final report soon after session 14. This report should **GOSP** the readers, that is *grab* their attention, *orient* them, move them along in *steps*, so they appreciate the *position* you have led them to.

Follow up

Writing and revising can seem like all-consuming activities. However, you should factor in time away from the text when solutions to expository problems can percolate to the surface. During that time you can also invent new avenues of classroom, workplace, or public participation, the goal of the **Phase I**.

Phase I—Engagement with Others

Goal

"I have facilitated new avenues of classroom, workplace, and public participation."

Background

By moving your research and writing towards completion (**Phase H**), you have established an invaluable basis for further *engagement*. That is, your writing is a basis for taking action to change your work, life, or wider social arrangements and building relationships with others in such action. In short, for taking action that combines head, heart, hands, and human connections. (Of course, the opportunity to reach out to others based on what you have been learning may arise at any time during your project. This phase is inserted after Compelling Communication because, with the end of writing in sight, you may be ready to pay more attention to outreach.)

Tools and Processes

Pilot run of activities and other group processes
Revision of activities and other group processes in light of feedback or evaluation
Plan for future development of activities or group processes
Plan future written and spoken presentations
Explore avenues of public participation
Define proposals for further engagement and action

Follow up

No elaboration or sequencing is given for the processes for Phase I, which are simply listed above to remind you of possibilities to start exploring even when your research and writing are not yet complete. A systematic framework to keep attention on engagement at every step of your research is provided by the **Cycles and Epicycles of Action Research**.

Phase J—Taking Stock

Goal

"To feed into my future learning and other work, I have taken stock of what has been working well and what needs changing."

Background

Reflective practitioners in any profession pilot new practices, take stock of outcomes and reflect on possible directions, and make plans to revise their practice accordingly. This phase is listed last because it is important not to move on from a project (or meeting, workshop, etc.) without making time to take stock of where you have come and what you might take into the next project. However, taking stock should occur from the very start of the project.

Tools and Processes

Support and Coaching Structure
Plus-Delta Feedback
Self-Assessment, Mid-Project
Sense of Place Map
Written Evaluation
Self-Assessment, at the End
Process Review

Sequence

Note: Most of these processes to take stock of your process over the course of the project not only feed back into your future learning but also contribute to your advisors (instructors) taking stock of how you have learned, which feeds back into their advising (teaching) and their future learning about how advisees (students) learn.

early in the course of the project
Discussion among a group of peers discussion with your peers about establishing a **Support and Coaching Structure** to get everyone to finish their research and writing in the time available.

during the project ("formative evaluation")
Although the **Self-Assessment at the End** with respect to Goals of Research and Engagement should be prepared and submitted with your final report, it is also useful to undertake this self-assessment along the way (using the simple **Plus-Delta feedback**) and to attach the latest version with each submission. If there are discrepancies between an advisor's assessment and what you submit, they can note this in their comments on the submission. The discrepancies can then be discussed and a shared understanding arrived at.

Mid-project (mid-semester) Self-assessment (This brief self-assessment of your project can be expanded to encompass a report on the gap between where you are and where you would like to be in relation to **Research Organization**—both on paper and on your computer—and research and study competencies [CCT 2010].)

at end of project
Standard evaluation forms are not very conducive to participants taking stock of their own process and contributions. Taking stock can be achieved in other ways that complement each other:
Sense of Place Map
Written Evaluation of the process or course that begins with a quick self-assessment (as distinct from the extended Self-Assessment below).
Process Review including annotations and cover note
Self-Assessment at the End with respect to two sets of goals:

> I. goals of **Phases** of Research and Engagement
> II. **Reflective Practitioner Goals**, including taking initiative in or through relationships

Share the self-assessment with your advisor(s). If there are big discrepancies between their assessment and your self-assessment, you should discuss the discrepancies and try to come to a shared understanding so as to inform the planning and conduct of your future projects.

Follow up

During the course of the project, you can refer back to the Plus of the Plus-Delta to reassure you about the progress you have made and to the Delta to remind yourself of changes to be made or tasks to be undertaken. Similarly, you can use the Self-Assessment at the End to inform the planning and conduct of your future projects. You can also ponder the Sense of Place Map, which you might pin on the wall above your work area. Although the thinking that went into the pictorial elements of that map may gradually be lost to you, that is nothing to worry about. Perhaps that simply means it is time to draw a new Sense of Place Map.

CYCLES and EPICYCLES of ACTION RESEARCH

Action Research begins when you (as an individual or as a group) want to do something to change the current situation, that is, to take *action*. "Action" can refer to many different things: a new or revised curriculum; a new organizational arrangement, policy, or procedure in educational settings; equivalent changes in other professions, workplaces, or communities; changes in personal practices, and so on. Action Research traditionally progresses from evaluations of previous actions through stages of planning and implementing some action to evaluation of its effects, that is, research to show what ways the situation after the action differs from the way it was before. This cycle of Action Research is conveyed in the following figure.

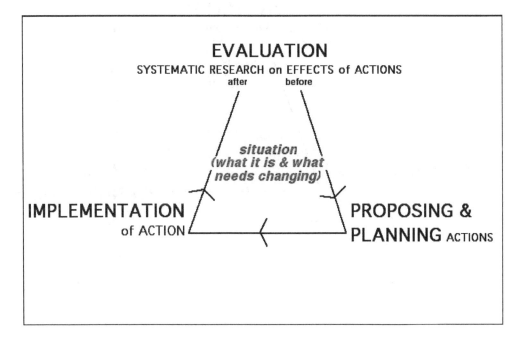

The basic cycle of Action Research

To this basic cycle of Action Research we can add *reflection and dialogue* through which you review and revise the ideas you have about what action is needed as well as your ideas about how to *build a constituency* to implement the change. Your thinking about what the situation is and what needs changing can also be altered by *inquiring into the background* (e.g., what motivates you to change this situation?) as well as looking ahead to future stages. Just like the basic cycle of Action Research, constituency building happens over time, so we can think of this a second cycle. The other additions above, however, often make us go back and revisit what had seemed clear and settled, so we can call these the *epicycles* (i.e., cycles on top of cycles) of Action Research. The composite of all these factors is conveyed in the following figure. (See also Taylor 2009 for a step-by-step presentation).

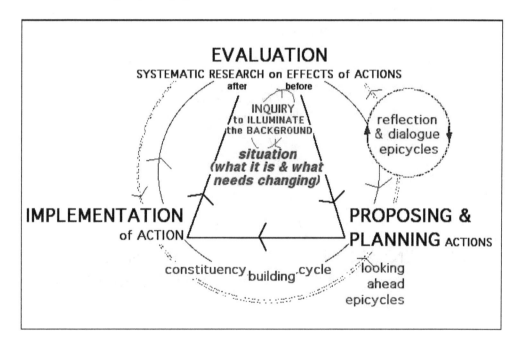

The Cycles and Epicycles of Action Research

Below we expand on this introduction then elaborate on the key aspects of Action Research. After that follows a list of tools and processes useful in the different aspects of Action Research. In Part 3 the use of various tools and processes is illustrated by excerpts from a semester-long project by Jeremy on designing Collaborative Play by Teachers in Curriculum Planning. We recognize that the exposition to follow is brief—a summary more than a detailed guide. We believe that the interplay between the cycles and epicycles will become clear primarily through experience conducting Action Research and through practice using the tools.

Elaboration on the Introduction to Action Research

Action Research begins, as noted above, when you (as an individual or as a group) want to do something to change the current situation, that is, to take action towards educational, organizational, professional, or personal change. (The complementary **Phases** framework emphasizes research and writing that prepares you to communicate with an audience.) To move from some broad idea of the action you think is needed to a more refined and do-able proposal, you may need to review *evaluations* of the effects of past actions (including possibly evaluations of actions you have previously made) and to conduct *background inquiry* so you can take into account other relevant considerations (e.g., who funds or sponsors these kinds of changes and evaluations). You also have to get people—yourself included—to adopt or adapt your proposals, that is, you have to build a constituency for any actions. *Constituency building* happens in a number of ways: when you draw people into *reflection*, *dialogue*, and other participatory processes in order to elicit ideas about the current situation, clarify objectives, and generate ideas and *plans* about taking action to improve the situation; when people work together to implement actions; and when people see *evaluations* of how good the actions or changes were in achieving the objectives. Evaluation of the effects of an action or change can lead to new or revised ideas about further changes and about how to build a constituency around them, thus stimulating ongoing cycles of Action Research.

These cycles are not a steady progression of one step to the next. Reflection and dialogue epicycles *at any point* in the cycle can lead to you to revisit and revise the ideas you had about what change is needed and about how to build a constituency to implement the change. Revision also happens when, before you settle on what actions to pursue, you move "backwards" and look at evaluations of past actions and conduct other background inquiry. Revision can also happen when you look ahead at what may be involved in implementing or evaluating proposed actions or in building a constituency around them. Such looking ahead is one of the essential features of planning.

In summary, Action Research involves evaluation and inquiry, reflection and dialogue, constituency building, looking ahead, and revision in order to clarify what to change, to get actions implemented, to take stock of the outcomes, and to continue developing your efforts.

Of course, as is the case with all evaluations and with research more generally, there is no guarantee that the results of Action Research will influence relevant people and groups (the so-called "stakeholders"). However, constituency building—including dialogue and reflection on the implications of the results—provides a good basis for mobilizing support and addressing potential opposition in the wider politics of applied research and evaluation.

Elaboration on the Aspects of Action Research

Evaluation is the systematic study of the effects of actions. Evaluations may be of actions taken before you got involved or in another setting as well as actions you implement. You can use evaluations to design new or revised actions and to convince others to implement equivalent actions in other settings. To establish the specific effect of a specific action you need to compare two situations—one in which the action is taken and one in which it is not, with nothing else varying systematically between the two situations. Such a comparison may be hard to find or achieve. In any case, tightly focused evaluations need to be complemented by broader *inquiry* to clarify for yourself what warrants change given what is known about this situation and others like it and to clarify what a potential constituency might be.

Constituency building involves getting others to adopt or adapt your action proposals, or, better still, enlisting others to become part of the "you" that shapes, evaluates, and revises any proposals. Adoption or adaptation is helped by succinct presentations to a potential constituency about the action proposals and the evaluations and inquiry that supports them. Enlistment of others is helped by well-facilitated participation of stakeholders in the initial evaluation and inquiry, in formulation of action proposals, and in planning so as to bring about their investment in implementing the proposals. If the actions are personal changes and the constituency is yourself, you can still facilitate your own evaluation and planning process to ensure your investment in the actions. Indeed, constituency building for any action begins with yourself. In order to contribute effectively to change, you need to be engaged—to have your head, heart, hands, and human connections aligned. You need to pay attention to what help you need to get engaged and stay so.

Reflection and dialogue happen in a variety of activities (see, e.g., tools useful for Action Research below and **Reflective Practitioner Goals**). However, the quality they share is making space to listen to yourself and others so that thoughts about an issue can emerge that had been below the surface of your attention or come into focus. Reflection and dialogue are valuable in Action Research for these reasons, among others: ongoing revision of your ideas about the current situation; generating action proposals; and drawing more people into your constituency. Through reflection and dialogue you can check that the evaluation and inquiry you undertake about the current situation and past actions relate well to possible actions you are considering and to the constituencies you intend to build. You can check that the results of your evaluations and inquiry support the actions and constituency building you pursue. You can review what actually happens when an action is implemented and its effects are evaluated and, on that basis, generate ideas for the next cycle of Action Research.

Planning involves looking ahead at what may be involved before you settle on what actions to pursue. Planning is strategic when action proposals respect the resources—possibly limited—that you and others in your constituency have and when the planning process elicits people's investment in implementation of those actions.

Tools and Processes Useful in the Different Aspects of Action Research

RD = Reflection and Dialogue
CB = Constituency building
EI = Evaluation and Inquiry
P = Planning

	RD	CB	EI	P
Check-In	RD	CB		
Closing Circle (Check-Out)	RD	CB		
Critical Incident Questionnaire			EI	
Dialogue Process	RD	CB		
Evaluation Clock (review of past evaluations)			EI	
Evaluation Clock (planning future evaluations)			EI	P
Focused Conversation	RD	CB		
Freewriting	RD			
Gallery Walk	RD	CB	EI	
Historical Scan	RD	CB		
Jigsaw Discussion of Texts	RD		EI	
KAQF	RD		EI	P
One-on-one Consultations within a Group	RD	CB		
Plus-Delta Feedback	RD	CB	EI	
Small-Group Roles	RD	CB		
Statistical Thinking			EI	
Strategic Personal Planning	RD			P
Supportive Listening	RD			
Think-Pair-Share	RD			

CREATIVE HABITS for SYNTHESIS of THEORY and PRACTICE

At various points in your life you may take up the challenge of writing something in which you synthesize your ideas and practice. After all, everyone has a voice that should be heard. However, believing deeply that your voice matters and acting on that belief is not easy. You will need support to be able to take yourself seriously and, as the title of Parker Palmer's (2000) book puts it, to "Let Your Life Speak." The frameworks of Phases and of the Cycles and Epicycles of Action Research together with the creative habits below provide a multifaceted structure to help you find your voice, clarify and develop your thoughts, express that voice in writing, and complete your synthesis of ideas and practice. The structure is especially valuable if you want to finish by some defined target date yet do not want to rely on external directions to motivate or reward you.

Frameworks

Phases of Research and Engagement, which includes

> **Dialogue around Written Work** and
> Developing as a **Reflective Practitioner**, which includes
> > **Taking Initiative In and Through Relationships**

Cycles and Epicycles of Action Research

Creative Habits

Establish support from:
- *yourself*—**Daily Writing**, a practice of expository writing 15-30 minutes 5-7 days per week from the very start of a project
- *a small group that meets regularly*—**Writing Groups for**

Support and Feedback

- *a larger group of peer writers*—**Writing Workshop**, to check in on progress and reflect on topics relevant to voice, synthesizing, writing, getting support, revising, and finishing.
- *your advisor*—**One-on-one Session**, which can be given a more mindful structure than the typically free-form discussions between researcher and advisor.

Your personal support systems should include some other creative habits and commitments:

- Make space in your life and domestic arrangements so you can undertake writing and engage in Writing Support Groups.
- Establish and maintain a bibliographic database for ready retrieval and formatting of references.
- Seek out guides or advisors in your area of specialization.
- Arrange an outside editor to help with revision and copy-editing. Do not expect your advisors to do this for you.

2
TOOLS & PROCESSES

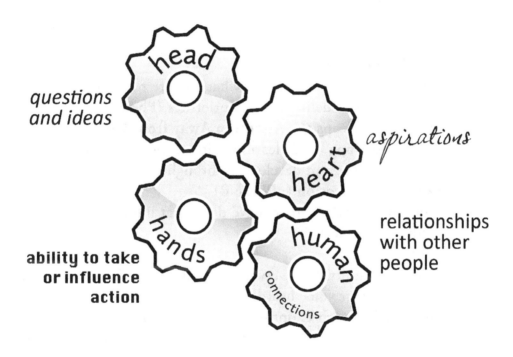

questions
and ideas

head

aspirations

heart

ability to take
or influence
action

hands

human

connections

relationships
with other
people

TOOLS and PROCESSES

The annotations below provide an entry point to the items listed. Phases in which items are introduced are indicated in parentheses. Full definitions and descriptions are given in separate entries that follow this list except, when the tools or processes correspond to a whole phase or framework, details can be found in Part 1, Phases, Cycles and Habits.

Active Digestion
> To ensure that what you read becomes part of your own thinking (Phase B)

Annotated Bibliography
> To check the significance of what you are reading against your current project definition and priorities (Phase B)

Assessment that Keeps the Attention Away from Grades
> Helps teaching and learning interactions focused on the student's process of developing through the semester

Background Information (=Phase B)
> Finding out what others have done that informs and connects with your project

Check-In
> An opportunity for every participant to begin to participate and have their voice heard

Clarification Through Communication (=Phase G)
> Overall progression or argument underlying your research and the written reports

Closing Circle (Check-Out)
> An opportunity for every participant to take stock of the session or their plan for the time ahead and to have this heard (witnessed) by the rest of the group

Compelling Communication (=Phase H)
> Drafting and revising writing so the result grabs the attention of the readers, orients them, and moves them along in steps so they appreciate the position you have led them to

Component Propositions (=Phase D) and Component Propositions—Teasing Out

Identify the propositions that your project depends on and the research needed to support those propositions (Phase D)

Creative Habits for Synthesis of Theory and Practice

Framework to establish a structure of support to find your voice, clarify and develop thoughts, and express that voice in a completed written product

Critical Incident Questionnaire

Five minute feedback that can be fitted in at the end of almost any session

Cycles and Epicycles of Action Research

Framework that emphasizes reflection and dialogue through which you revisit and revise the ideas you have about what action is needed and about how to build a constituency to implement the change

Daily Writing

A practice of writing 15-30 minutes 5-7 days per week from the very start of a project

Design of Further Research and Engagement (=Phase E)

Clear objectives with respect to product and process, in sequence of steps

Dialogue around Written Work

Written and spoken comments on each installment of a project and successive revision in response facilitates generative interactions between researcher and advisor

Dialogue Process

Shared and personal meaning that emerges within a group discussion through listening, inquiry, and reflection

Direct Information, Models, and Experience (=Phase F)

Information, models, and experience not readily available from other sources

Direct Writing and Quick Revising

Split the time you have available into two: write complete sentences, then put what you have in order (Phase H)

Drafts (Narrative, Complete, Final)

building on a narrative outline, proceed directly to a complete draft of your report (or through the intermediate step of a narrative draft) then revise in response to comments to produce a final report

Engagement with Others (=Phase I)

Facilitating new avenues of classroom, workplace, and public participation

Evaluation Clock (to plan evaluations)

A framework to design your own evaluation or systematic study, working both sequentially and recursively

Evaluation Clock (to review completed evaluations)

Learn to plan evaluations by using the Clock to and identify the steps taken in a completed evaluation

Five F's

Background research involves a continuing interplay among Find, Focus, Filter, Face Fears, and File (Phase B)

Focused Conversation

A series of questions that begin with concrete things you observed and move through feelings and associations, on to interpretations and finally get to the overall implications

Freewriting

Write non-stop for seven to ten minutes to expose thoughts about the topic that had been below the surface of your attention

Gallery Walk

Activity for a group's first meeting that introduces participants to each other and acknowledges that they already know a lot about the topic at hand

GOSP (Grab->Orient->Steps->Position)

Grab the attention of the readers or audience, Orient them, move them along in Steps, so they appreciate the Position you've led them to (Phase H)

Governing Question

Focuses you on what you need to find out that you do not already know or cannot yet demonstrate to someone else

Historical Scan

Review a group's progress or set the scene in which a project is to be undertaken

Initial Guide

Someone to guide your inquiries in their early unformed stage (Phase B)

Interview Guide

So you set the scene clearly, do not forget essential things, and have a checklist of items you wanted to cover

Jigsaw Discussion of Texts

Allows all members of a group to get up to steam on issues raised by a set of readings without everyone having read every reading in depth

KAQF

Identify what you need to Find out by examining the interplay between Knowledge, Questions for inquiry, and ideas about possible Actions

Key Article

Points to many other publications and so moves you towards the goal of knowing what others have done that informs and connects with your project (Phase B)

Making Space for Taking Initiative in and through Relationships

Focus on a few reflective practitioner goals at any given time, but keep the other considerations in mind and address any tensions among them

Mapping

Tease out connections from the central issue that concerns you (Phase C)

Models from the Past

Review reports from previous projects to get a sense of their scope and the look of the final products (Phase A)

Narrative Outline

Outline with explanatory sentences that indicate the point of each section and interconnections among sections (Phase G)

One-on-one Session

Discussions between researcher and advisors are typically free-form, but can be given a more mindful structure

One-on-one Consultations within a Group

Opportunities to solicit advice one on one during a meeting or workshop when there is 45-60 minutes to spare

Overall Argument—Clarification

What are the steps or progression that leads your audience to the position you want them at least to appreciate? (Phase G)

Paragraph Overview

A single paragraph to orient readers to your project as a whole (Phase A).

Personal and Professional Development Workbook

An organized compilation of materials to facilitate review of and later re-engagement with your thinking and processes of development

Phases of Research and Engagement

Framework of ten phases that researchers move through and, in a process of iterative development, revisit in light of other people's responses to their work and of what they learn during the other

Plus-Delta Feedback

Feedback in the form of an appreciation (plus) and a suggestion for change (delta)

Possible Directions and Priorities (=Phase C)

Expose possible new directions and clarify direction and scope within the larger set of issues

Process Review

Selected examples with annotations that capture the process of development of your work and thinking about the subject of the project or course (Phase J)

Pyramid of Questions

A compilation of questions arising during your research, with later questions building on earlier ones (Phase C)

Questions for Opening Wide and for Probing

Where? Who is implicated? Tease open arguments, categories, definitions, holes, and ambiguities (Phase C)

Reflective Practitioner Goals

Emphasizing taking initiative in and through relationships (Phase J)

Research Design

From reflection on your wider vision and obstacles to a sequence of achievable steps (Phase J)

Research Organization

Keep your ears and eyes open to good ideas, but customize the development of your research organization to your own situation and foibles

Reverse Outlining

After making a note on the topic(s) or thesis(theses) of each paragraph, see how these can be rearranged, streamlined, discarded, combined, split, so that each paragraph makes a distinct contribution to a definite GOSPing path (Phase H)

Revision

You should not expect to work out your ideas in one attempt —everyone needs to revise!

Self-Assessment, Mid-Project

What you like about your work so far. What you plan to do differently. Support you need for this (Phase J)

Self-Assessment, at the End

Describe for each specified goal (e.g., the goals of the Phases) one thing that reflects what you have achieved well related to this goal and one thing that you have struggled with, need more help on, or want to work further on (Phase J)

Sense-Making

Form of contextualization that teases out what has helped you and what has hindered you (Phase B)

Sense-Making Response

An approach to Active Digestion of what you are reading based on Sense-Making (Phase B)

Sense of Place Map

A picture that addresses: Where are you? Where have you come from? Where are you going?

Sharing of Work to Elicit Responses

Sharing as giving so that responses be elicited and offered from a place of mutual respect

Small-Group Roles

Roles that do not divert anyone from participating in a small-group activity and in which everyone has to reflect and synthesize what happened

Statistical Thinking

A simple chain of thinking to be understood before enlisting a statistician to analyze the data

Strategic Personal Planning

Acknowledging a wide range of factors and wishes that your work could take into account (Phase E)

Subject-Purpose-Audience (=Phase A)

Who you want to reach? What you want to convey to them? Why do *you* want to address them about that?

Support and Coaching Structure

Consider ways that the group can function as a support and coaching structure to get most participants (students) to finish their research and writing by the target date (Phase J)

Supportive Listening

Each person has half the time available to be listened to and simply paid attention to even if not talking

Taking Stock (=Phase J)

What has been working well and what needs changing—start early in the project and repeat often

Ten Questions, for Opening Wide then Focusing

Write down 10 questions then circle two that interest you the most. Take these two and list 10 questions under each (Phase C)

Think-Pair-Share

Prepare your thoughts on your own, share with a second person, then with group as a whole

Visual Aids

Aid your presentation, not duplicate it (Phase G)

Work-in-Progress Presentation

Through preparation, delivery, and feedback clarify your overall argument and plans for subsequent research (Phase G)

Writing Groups for Support and Feedback

A small group protects a regular meeting time and takes turns to give and receive feedback on the latest installment of writing

Writing Preferences

When you see your strengths you may keep that in mind as a

resource. When you see your weakness, you may do remedial exercises to try to reduce that as a liability (Phases G and H)

Writing Workshop

Regular hour-long writing workshop to check in on progress and reflect on relevant topics

Written Evaluation, at End of a Project or Course

Starting with a quick self-evaluation and moving through steps towards composing a synthetic statement aimed at helping the advisor (or instructor) and some third party appreciate the strengths and weaknesses of the process (or course) (Phase J)

Active Digestion

To digest the food you eat is for it to become part of your own body. Similarly, you have digested what you read when it becomes part of your own thinking. This requires some active strategy, such as the following:

- *Dialogue:* Make notes in which you have your own dialogue with the author. (You might put the dialogue notes in brackets next to [or on a page facing] any notes you record in your notebook.) Such dialogue helps you to get clear about the following: What was argued? What was not? Where could it have been taken further? Where does all this connect with my project?
- *Annotation:* For the important articles write a summary or annotation that indicates how the article relates to your project. Compiling an **Annotated Bibliography** not only provides bits of text to use when you write your report, but also forces you to push your own thinking further and convert what you are reading into your own material.
- ***Sense-Making*** *response*

Active Digestion is essential for making progress in your project in light of the **5 F's**. It is easy to Find and download more articles than you have time to read. Instead of reading all of every article or getting overwhelmed and giving up, you need to Filter out readings that might seem interesting but are not important given your evolving Focus. Through Active Digestion of what you do read, you can refine your Focus.

(see **Phase B**)

Annotated Bibliography

As you compile a list of reading completed or planned, *annotate* the list to indicate the relevance of the article or book chapter to your topic. Annotating your Bibliography serves several functions:
• You take stock of the significance of the reading in light of your current project definition and priorities;
• You provide your advisors and other readers with a basis to help you identify holes and any mismatch between what you are reading and your **Governing Question**; and
• You compose sentences that may find their way into your writing.

When choosing what to include in the bibliography, quantity is less important than a clear relationship of the readings to the evolving focus of your project. There is no need to pack or pad the bibliography with zillions of references uncovered in your searches. Instead, use the compilation of a bibliography to stimulate the process of clarifying whether and in what ways an article is relevant to your project (see **Active Digestion**). Omit readings that no longer relate to the current direction of your project.

Because your topic might have changed or should be more concise by the time you submit this bibliography to your advisor, take stock of that and begin with a revised single **Paragraph Overview** of the current topic and Governing Question. Writing a tighter overview statement will also help to expose changes, gaps, and ambiguities. Comments by others on your initial statement also help, allowing that you can ignore comments rendered irrelevant by changes in your direction.

Consult a writing manual (e.g., Turabian 2007) to decide on a citation style, then use this consistently as you compile your bibliography—You do not have time to redo citations later.

(see **Phase B**)

Assessment that Keeps the Attention Away from Grades

To keep the attention away from grades during the semester, students can be told that they will be given an automatic grade, say, B+ at the end of the semester for satisfactory completion of 80% of the writing assignments—satisfactory meaning no further revision and resubmission requested—and for fulfillment of 80% of participation or process items. (Written assignments could be steps in the development of the major project for the course. Participation items could include prepared attendance at each session of the course, required **One-on-one Sessions** with the instructor (office hour meetings), maintaining a **Personal and Professional Development Workbook**, peer review of drafts, and so on.)

The practice of not grading any assignments or participation items is intended to keep teaching-learning interactions focused on the student's process of development through the semester. It is not an alternative to assessment, but matches an alternative form of assessment, namely, **Dialogue Around Written Work**. In that spirit, not grading during the semester frees up time and space for the student and instructor to appreciate and learn from what each other is saying and thinking. (Even more time is freed up if students use an assignment checklist to keep track of their own progress so the instructor does not have to remind them of overdue submissions or respond to the "can you tell me what my grade is so far?" question.)

The instructor makes clear that their goal is to work with each student to achieve the 80% level. (The 20% slack means students do not have to seek approval for any tactical decisions they make in light of competing priorities in their work, lives, and other courses.) Students who progress steadily towards the automatic grade level during the semester usually end up producing work that meets criteria for a higher grade. Such criteria could include:

• A sequence of assignments paced more or less as in syllabus, often revised thoroughly and with new thinking in response to comments.

• A project that is innovative, well planned and carried out with considerable initiative, and indicates that the student can guide others to think critically about the subject of the course.

• A project report that is clear and well structured, with supporting references and detail, and professionally presented.

• Active, prepared participation in all sessions of the course.

• Completion of most preparatory and follow-up homework tasks.

• A **Process Review** that shows deep reflection by the student on their development through the semester and maps out the future directions in which they plan to develop.

If the 80% level automatic grade is a B+, students who meet half the criteria well (or all the criteria moderately) would earn an A-. Students who show almost all the criteria well would earn an A. Students can be invited to submit their own self-assessment in relation to these criteria. If there is a significant discrepancy, the instructor and student should discuss that.

For students who do not meet the 80% level automatic grade, points can be awarded for each written assignment and participation item satisfactorily completed. For example, if the automatic grade is equal to 80 points and the course had 10 written assignments for 2/3 of the course grade and 20 participation items for 1/3 of the course grade, then each written assignment could count 6.67 points and each participation item 1.67 points. (Students can use such a points system to tally their grade during the semester. However, doing this runs against the intention of this assessment-without-grades system, so this possibility should not be emphasized.)

Check-In

During a Check-In, which may be a routine way to start a session, everyone is given a limited time, say, 1 minute, to speak to a prompt given by the session leader. A participant can pass and be given a turn at the end. If someone finishes speaking well under the allotted time, the leader can repeat the prompt, which usually elicits from the participant interesting additional thoughts. The prompts need not be directly related to the agenda of the session— the important point is that every participant begins to participate and have their voice heard.

Examples of Prompts

"Something new and good since the last session. (It doesn't have to be about the project [course].)"

"Progress and insights gained since the last session. (Do not say what you did *not* do. Mention what you did do and share any insights you gained about getting the other things done from this point on.)"

Closing Circle (Check-Out)

During a Closing Circle or Check-Out at the end of a session, everyone takes a turn to speak to a prompt given by the session leader. A volunteer starts, then that person is asked to pass it to their left or their right, and things then proceed round the circle (or group) in that direction. A participant can pass and be given a turn at the end.

The prompt should request that the responses are short, even telegraphic. The leader can gently thank someone to cut them off if they speak for too long, go beyond the prompt, or start to repeat themselves. The important point is that every participant takes stock of the session or their plan for the time ahead and that this is heard and witnessed by the rest of the group.

Examples of Prompts

Plus-Delta review of the session

One thing I am planning to do differently this week.

One thing that I plan to do this week and one thing I am taking away to chew on from this session.

Component Propositions—Teasing Out

There are usually a range of propositions underlying your research. These need to be identified and research done to support them. If support is lacking, you need to rethink their role in your project. To identify areas where additional thinking and research is needed, it often helps to presenting the propositions and corresponding counter-propositions to others who probe and discuss your thinking.

Consider, for example, a project with the following **Governing Question**:

> What aspects of my ongoing intellectual development become clear as I investigate the visceral impact of 19th Century American Romanticism on post-colonial New England and the importance of revisiting this history to understand who we are today as readers and writers.

This project rests on the propositions such as "American Romanticism had a visceral impact on post-colonial New England" and "our intellectual history (as Americans) is important to revisit in order to know who we are as readers and writers today." Evidence is needed to support the first proposition, but it is possible to re-express the second proposition so it does not require support: "It is important to me to revisit our intellectual history (as Americans) to know who we are as readers and writers today, where 'we' refers to me and to readers who are like me in sharing this premise." The proposition has become a premise. Readers who need to be convinced of this proposition are excluded from the audience, which may be OK with the researcher for this project. If that is so, this would be an illustration of "rethink the role of a proposition in your project."

In order to tease out what research is needed to support a proposition, it is helpful to identify counter-propositions and counter-counter-propositions. Continuing the example above, in the case of the first proposition the researcher identified the following:

Counter proposition—As an intellectual movement, American Romanticism only impacted the well-educated, wealthier, Anglo contingency of post-colonial New Englanders.

Counter-counter propositions:

1. While this movement did attract its share of wealthy, well-educated individuals, many of the contributors to the American Renaissance were home-schooled or poor.

2. Those it did impact reached out to others in the spirit of sharing learning and enlightenment.

3. This movement had a great visceral impact on my family who, while well educated, were farmers and trade workers living in Connecticut.

The lines of evidence that the researcher brought to bear to support the counter-propositions began from the following points:

1. Hawthorne, Thoreau, the Peabodys, and the Alcotts were constantly engaged in a battle with poverty. Their great faith in their art and learning gave them the power to keep producing literature or improving education.

2. Consider the case of Thomas Mann who almost died visiting county schools throughout New England in order to research and develop the best public school model possible—which he did when he established the Boston Public Schools.

3. My ancestors' concern and passion for 19th Century literature is evident in their letters that remain.

The inquiries implied in these initial points did not form central strands of the researcher's project, but spending some time on them enabled her to include in her audience any readers who might have needed convincing that 19th Century American Romanticism had a strong impact on post-colonial New England.

TOOLS AND PROCESSES

If the teasing out of propositions and counter-propositions is not yielding anything new, that is, no lines of inquiry where you do not already know the answer, you need to ask someone to probe your thinking. It may be that you are overlooking propositions underlying your projects that you have taken for granted or that you think are self-evident. The helper can take each branch or angle in your **Map** and ask you, "Is there any controversy here?" They can also question each proposition you have identified by asking, "Would anyone else formulate this in a different way?" The other person can play the devil's advocate and try to see the issues in a different way from you. Of course, when no other person is available, you can try to take the probing and devil's advocate roles for yourself.

Component Propositions could also be called component *arguments* but note that they operate at a different level from the **Overall Argument** of your writing or your **GOSP**, that is, how you grab people's attention, orient them, move them along in steps, so that they appreciate the position at each step that you've taken them to. Indeed, teasing out Component Propositions can come at an earlier point than clarifying your Overall Argument or GOSP, which is important when you begin to outline or draft your report. At this earlier point, the idea is to identify the variety of small and large propositions that are implicated in your project, tease out and prioritize the research needed to support them, and, if you are not able to gather support for some propositions, rethink their role in your project.

See **Phase D**.

Critical Incident Questionnaire

A Critical Incident Questionnaire (Brookfield 1995, 115) is designed to elicit written reactions in a short period at the end of a session. Setting a limit of five minutes for this feedback means that use of the Questionnaire can be fitted in to almost any session and, because each person's responses are necessarily partial, there is no pressure on a person to sum up the whole experience. The session leader (e.g., instructor) can collate the responses onto a single sheet (using check marks to indicate repeats of similar responses) and annotate the results, e.g., highlighting repeated responses, linking items in tension (i.e., when respondents said opposite things), and summarizing a manageable subset of issues to address next time. This compilation can be scanned and sent by email with a cover note or distributed the next session accompanied by a short spoken recap of the highlights.

The sequence of questions in the examples below borrows from the **Focused Conversation**, which moves participants from the *objective* (concrete things, actually observable by all), through *reflective* (associations and feelings) and *interpretive* (meaning and significance) to *decisional* (implications for the future) (Stanfield 1997).

Example

Please take about 5 minutes to respond anonymously to each of the questions below about tonight's session. Using the carbon paper, make one copy for yourself and put the other by the door as you leave. I'll digest the responses, report back to you next week about them, and try to make changes that address your responses.

1. What incident/comment/reaction/quote stands out from tonight's session?

2. At what moment did you feel most:

    a. engaged with what was happening?
    b. distanced from what was happening?

3. What action that anyone (teacher or student) took did you find:

    a. most helpful or affirming?
    b. most puzzling or confusing?

4 (Optional). Other comments?

Another example, for mid-way during a semester

1. What concrete incidents/comments/reactions in tonight's session caught your attention?

2a. What excited you?

b. What frustrated you?

3a. What trends do you see emerging in the sessions?

b. What are the implications of these for your learning and thinking?

4a. What might be your next steps as a learner-participant in this project (course)?

b. What support would you like in taking those steps?

Daily Writing

A practice of writing text related to your project 15-30 minutes five to seven days per week (Boice 1990, Gray n.d.). Log time spent and new words written, and, at the end of each session, note possible topics for future Daily Writing. *New words* is important—editing, revising, and filling in citations can be done at another time in the day. Indeed, daily writing should lead to a release of energy for other research and writing work entailed by your project.

Start Daily Writing at the very start of your project. The words you write need not ever end up in the final written product, so it does not matter if your project is unclear at the start and changes as you go on. Note, however, that Daily Writing differs from **Freewriting** or Cameron's (2002) "Morning Pages." Your Daily Writing words should be expository, composed as if you are presenting some points to an audience.

Dialogue around Written Work

Dialogue around Written Work refers to written and spoken comments on each installment of a project, revision in response to those comments, and comments on the revisions. What the advisor needs the advisee to hear (or the instructor needs the student to hear) to get them comfortable with this process:

> I try to create a dialogue with each advisee (student) around written work, that is, around your writing, my responses, and your responses in turn. For each submission I make comments on a cover page that aim to show you your voice has been heard and to reflect back to you where you were taking me. After the overall comments I make specific suggestions for how to clarify and extend the impact on readers of what was written. I usually ask you to revise and resubmit the submission. The goal is not that you make changes to please me as the advisor (instructor) or to meet some unstated standard, but that you as a writer use the eye of others to develop your own thinking and make your written exposition of that thinking work better on readers. I may continue to request revision when I judge that the interaction can still yield significant learning. Such a request does not mean your (re)submission was *bad*. Even when first submissions of written submissions are excellent, angles for learning through dialogue are always opened up.

> I hope my comments capture where you were taking me and that my suggestions help you see how to clarify and extend the impact on readers of what you have written. However, after letting my comments sink in, you may conclude that I have missed your point. In that case, my misreading may stimulate you to revise so as to help readers avoid mistaking

the intended point. However, if you do not understand the directions I saw in your work or those that I suggest for the revision, a **One-on-one Session**, face-to-face or by phone, is the obvious next step. I say this in recognition of the definite limitations of written comments when writers and readers want to appreciate and learn from what each other is saying and thinking. Indeed, please arrange a One-on-one Session without delay if you do not see how you are benefiting from the process of revision and resubmission.

To students: I recognize that Dialogue around Written Work departs from most students' expectations of "produce a product one time only and receive a grade." And I know that most students at first are uncomfortable exposing their work and engaging in extended dialogue over it. So I continue to look for ways to engage students in this process that take into account your various backgrounds and dispositions.

As part of Dialogue around Written Work, your advisors (or instructors) can assemble a portfolio of your installments and comments. They can then review these when making new comments, which should enhance their interactions with you. Their comments—even when they are not an expert in your project's topic—are more likely to be generative, that is, to help you to bring to the surface, form, and articulate your ideas as a researcher.

Dialogue Process

The Dialogue Process centers around listening—to yourself as well as others. Shared and personal meaning emerges within a group through listening to what is said from a standpoint of inquiry and reflection (Isaacs 1999).

What follows are detailed and then streamlined scripts for a Dialogue Process session in which the participants learn about the process as we go. (These scripts build on those of Bradford 1999.)

Detailed Script

[Facilitator speaks:] Dialogue Process session on *[facilitator fills in topic]*
Pass this sheet around, each person reading one paragraph of a script prepared by Allyn Bradford and Peter Taylor.

Background

In the Dialogue Process *meaning* evolves collectively through mutual understanding and acceptance of diverse points of view.

To master the Dialogue Process requires learning a variety of communication skills including a tolerance of paradox (or opposing views), the suspension of judgment, and empathetic listening. It also requires making the entire thought process visible, including tacit assumptions. In this process, instead of imposing our views on others, we invite others to add new dimensions to what we are thinking. We also learn to listen to the voice of the heart—our own and others—and strive to find ways to make that voice articulate.

The purpose of dialogue is neither to agree nor to determine who is right. Rather, the purpose is to discover the richness of diverse perceptions that create a shared meaning that emerges from a group through inquiry and reflection. The meaning that evolves is dynamic as it moves through many diverse phases. If others contradict, the challenge is to learn from what they have said.

The origin of dialogue goes back to the ancient Greeks. It is also found among preliterate Europeans and Native Americans. More recently David Bohm, the renowned physicist introduced the Dialogue Process into the scientific quest for knowledge and also used it to address social problems. Bohm said that "when the roots of thought are observed, thought itself seems to change for the better." Dialogue, he said, "is a stream of meaning flowing among and through and between us." Dialogue is now being used in schools, corporations and government to develop rapport, resolve conflict, and build community.

Guidelines

1. You don't have to agree. Listen with the expectation of learning —that is, assume that the speaker has something new and of value to contribute to your comprehension and then stretch your mind to find out what that is.

2. None of us has the whole truth. Seek to comprehend the many facets of meaning that emerge from the group. Appreciate how the diversity of perceptions enriches the quality of the dialogue. In your responses do not problem solve, argue, analyze, rescue, nit pick or give advice. Rather, try to understand how the diverse views connect with each other.

3. Pay attention to your listening. Listen for the "voice of the heart" as well as the mind—yours and others'. Tune into the language, rhythms and sounds. Listen as you would to hear the themes played by various instruments in an orchestra and how they relate to each other. That's what makes the music. In Dialogue, that is what makes the collective meaning.

4. Free yourself up from a rigid mindset. Stand back and respond, rather than reacting automatically or defensively. Balance advocacy (making a statement) with inquiry (seeking clarifications and understanding). In advocating do not impose your opinion, rather simply offer it as such. In inquiry seek clarification and a deeper level of understanding, not the exposure of weakness.

5. Communicate your reasoning process, i.e., talk about your assumptions and how you arrived at what you believe. Seek out the data on which assumptions are based, your own and others. Bring tacit (hidden) assumptions to the surface of consciousness.

6. Suspend, rather than identify with, your judgements. Hold these away from your core self, to be witnessed or observed by yourself and made visible to others.

7. *Confidentiality:* Do not speak afterwards about what is said in the dialogue by attributing it to anyone, even if you don't name the person. Instead, simply talk about what you are thinking or inquiring about as a result of having been in today's session. If you speak to anyone from this group about what they said, follow the same genuine inquiry you practice here.

8. *Turn-taking:* The overriding idea: Keep focused on listening well. You won't listen well if you are thinking about whether you will get to talk next or are holding on tight to what you want to say. So take a numbered card when you feel that you would like a turn, but keep listening. When your turn comes, show your card, and pause. See if you have something to follow what is being said, even if it is not the thought you had wanted to say. You can pass.

There is no need for questions to be answered right away. If the question relates directly to someone, they can pick it up when they next take a turn. This differs from usual conversations, but think of questions as inquiries that you are putting into a shared space.

Try to make the turn-taking administer itself so the facilitator can listen well and participate without distraction. When you finish speaking (or if you decide to pass), put your card on the stack of used cards so the person with the next card knows that they can begin. The facilitator's role becomes simply to recharge the unused stack of cards when needed and gently remind people to follow the guidelines.

Check-in

Go around the circle with each person saying one thought that's at the front for you as we go into the session.
[Stop passing the sheet around at this point, and take turns in checking-in.]

[Facilitator speaks:]

Turn-taking dialogue about the topic at hand for the time available

[Facilitator reminds group of the topic]
* * * *

[Facilitator closes off the turn-taking so as to keep the last 8+ minutes for the last two phases of the Dialogue]

Writing to gather thoughts from what has emerged

Two-three minutes for each of us to write.

Check-out

Go around the circle with each person saying one thought that you are taking away to chew on after this session.

Streamlined Script

Dialogue Process session on [*facilitator fills in topic*]
Guidelines: Pass this sheet around, each person reading one paragraph of guidelines from Allyn Bradford and Peter Taylor

The Dialogue Process is an opportunity to listen—not only to the thinking of others, but also to our own thoughts and feelings that had been below the surface of our attention.

When a group does this together over a period of time, *meaning* emerges and evolves collectively through mutual understanding and acceptance of diverse points of view. In this short session, however, we cannot expect this to be the dominant experience.

The Dialogue Process works well when participants tolerate paradox and opposing views, suspend judgment, and listen empathetically, and try to make their entire thought process visible, including tacit assumptions. Instead of imposing our views on others, we invite others to add new dimensions to what we are thinking, and strive to find ways to make unexpressed or under-expressed voices articulate.

In this spirit, balance advocacy—making a statement—with inquiry —seeking clarifications and understanding. In advocating do not impose your opinion, rather simply offer it as such. In inquiry seek clarification and a deeper level of understanding, not the exposure of weakness.

The Dialogue Process requires structured turn-taking. The overriding idea is to keep focused on listening well. You won't listen well if you are thinking about whether you will get to talk next or are holding on tight to what you want to say.

Take a numbered card when you feel that you would like a turn, but keep listening. When your turn comes, show your card, and pause. See if you have something to follow what is being said, even if it is not the thought you had wanted to say. You can pass.

There is no need for questions to be answered right away. If the question relates directly to someone, they can pick it up when they next take a turn. This differs from usual conversations, but think of questions as inquiries that you are putting into a shared space.

Try to make turn-taking administer itself so the facilitator can listen well and participate without distraction. When you finish speaking (or if you decide to pass), put your card on the stack of used cards so the person with the next card knows that they can begin. The facilitator's role becomes simply to gently remind people to follow the guidelines.

Check-in: Go around the circle with each person saying one thought that is at the front for you before we go into the session proper. This need not be about the topic of the session.

[Stop passing the sheet around at this point, and take turns in checking-in.]

[Facilitator reminds participants of the topic, then we move to]
Turn-taking dialogue about the topic for the time available
* * * *

[Facilitator closes off the turn-taking so as to keep the last 8+ minutes for the last two phases of the Dialogue]
Writing to gather thoughts from what has emerged: Two-three minutes for each of us to write.

Check-out: Go around the circle with each person saying one thought that you're taking away to chew on after this session.

Direct Writing and Quick Revising

Split the time you have available for writing into two. Use the first half to write complete sentences, but not to do fine-tuning. This is the Direct Writing part. Use the second half to do the Quick Revising:

- Find a suitable order for the sentences (e.g., by numbering them).
- Add any necessary transitional sentences.
- Tidy up what you have.

The resulting text may be short, but it is a coherent product that is finished. (This technique comes from Elbow 1981, chapters 4 and 5.)

(see **Phase H**)

Drafts (Narrative, Complete, Final)

Ideally, a **Narrative Outline** should provide a sufficient scaffold for you to proceed directly to a complete draft of your report, but sometimes the intermediate step of a narrative draft is needed. To progress from a complete draft to the final report, all writers need to **Revise** in response to **Sharing of Work**. **Reverse Outlining** may be needed if a draft report does not **GOSP** readers well. The drafts and final report should not be directed to the advisor or instructor, but to the relevant audience that you would like to influence or to peer readers. Ask yourself what would this audience needs to know to get interested in your project and understand what you have done.

Narrative Draft

A narrative draft expands on the **Narrative Outline**, focusing first on the explanatory sentences that indicate the point of each section (and subsection) and interconnections among sections. Once that is clear, topic sentences for paragraphs become the next priority. Text can then be added into the paragraphs. At each stage, keep checking whether the paragraphs each have a distinct point, flow one to the next, and speak to the topic of the section that the paragraphs are in.

Complete Draft

For a draft to be complete you have to get to the end, even if you only sketch some sections along the way. An incomplete draft usually leaves readers—and yourself—unsure if you are clear about the position you want to lead them to and can fill in all the steps needed to get them there (see **GOSP**).

Final Report

Whatever form your report on a project takes, it should **GOSP** the readers, that is, *grab* their attention, *orient* them, move them along in *steps*, so they appreciate the *position* you have led them to. There are two aspects to orienting readers: foreshadow the expository steps ahead, and give readers a sense of why *you* are someone they should be interested in listening to on the topic. On this latter point, you might convey why you have pursued this project, your process of development during the project, and your personal or professional development plans for the future. (This might be informed by **Sense-Making** contextualization.)

Cite references consistently in the text and in a bibliography (which is sometimes labeled Works Cited or References). Only references that you have cited in the text should be in the bibliography, but you might include a supplementary bibliography of references used but not cited if that seems helpful to readers. It is not customary to include annotations of references cited in the report—the text of the report should indicate the relevance of the reference—but you might include annotations of references included in a supplementary bibliography. For a guide on technical matters of writing scholarly papers, see a writing manual such as Turabian (2007).

Evaluation Clock

The Evaluation Clock (adapted from Pietro 1983) unpacks the evaluation or systematic study component of the **Cycles and Epicycles of Action Research** framework. The Clock indirectly addresses the planning component of the framework by making you look ahead to consider which people might be influenced by the results and what they could do based on the possible outcomes.

The ultimate goal of using the Clock framework is that you can use it to design your own evaluation or systematic study mindfully, working not only
• *sequentially*—addressing the whole range of considerations (moving from steps 0 to 11)—but also
• *recursively*—adjusting your plans for the earlier steps in light of thinking ahead about possibilities for the later steps.
In particular, evaluation and planning (or design) should be inextricably linked. For example, when you think about what could be done differently (step 11) on the basis of the specific measurements or observations you include in the evaluation (step 3), you may refine your measurements or observations. You may even decide to separate out two or more different sub-issues within the overall issue (steps 0-2), each requiring a different evaluation. As Pietro (1983, 23) says: "The clock marks time in an unusual fashion, since it does not necessarily move in a clockwise direction, but rather jumps from one number to another until all the questions have been struck." It has been suggested that using the Clock looks more like undoing a safe's combination lock. Working sequentially and recursively is characteristic of Action Research as a whole, except that with the Evaluation Clock each step might require a tight, self-conscious method (see, e.g., **Statistical Thinking**).

Comparisons

When the evaluation is a systematic study of effects of some intervention or engagement, there is always a comparison involved. The comparison might be *before* versus *after* some intervention is made, or it might be a comparison of one situation (where a particular curriculum, treatment, etc. is used) versus another situation (lacking that curriculum, etc.) (steps 2 and 3 of the Clock). Did the intervention have the intended effects? Was it better than other approaches? (The idea of comparison can also be applied to continuous data, e.g., on the incidence of violent crimes in relation to unemployment rate. This is, more or less, equivalent to asking is there more (or less) violent crime in times of high unemployment than in times of low unemployment?)

In valid comparisons all other factors are supposed to be equal or unchanged. If they are not, then the comparison is suspect. Perhaps it needs to be broken into a number of comparisons, e.g., before versus after for privileged schools, and before versus after for poor schools.

When the evaluation is a systematic study of what has already been happening, it may only involve collecting information about one situation, e.g., finding what percentage of adults are able to read competently. The formulation of the evaluation criteria and interpretation of the results depends, however, on an implicit comparison with a desired situation, e.g., one in which there is full adult literacy.

Learning to use the Clock

In order to get acquainted with the comparison at the heart of the Clock and the sequential and recursive aspects of using it, it is helpful to reconstruct an evaluation that has already been conducted. When you do this you have to imagine being one of the people who did the research and fill in the steps they appear to have taken. In order to get the hang of comparisons, start by focusing on steps 2 and 3 for a simple case (e.g., Goode 1998 on the effects of a smoking in bars). Steps 0, 4 and 5 may help you as well. (These steps make up the stripped down clock appended below the full Clock.) When you have the hang of the comparison idea, then pay attention to the sequential and recursive aspects of the Clock.

The *sequential* part of reconstructing an evaluation means that the answers at each step are logically related to the previous ones, especially the immediately preceding one. For example, the lessons in step 10 are lessons learned from the reasons (step 9) for what is happening (step 8a). Similarly, the outlets (step 8b) should take into account the sponsors' goals and audience (step 1). Sequentiality also means that the key issues of the evaluation (step 2) cannot be the issues that emerge *after* the results (steps 8-12). The key issues must be what the evaluators saw needed studying before they knew the actual results.

The *recursive* part of reconstructing an evaluation means that when you think about what the evaluators or their sponsors did with the results (steps 10 and 11)—or what they could conceivably do with the results—you might go back and revise your interpretation of what decisions or policies or actions were at stake (steps 0 and 1). For example, an evaluation that points out that a low percentage of New York City high school students were passing the Regents exam says little about causes of the low percentage or about ways to improve education in the school system. We might even suspect that what concerns the sponsors of the evaluation (step 0) was to discredit public education. This conjecture would have to be validated, of course. in the meantime, however, we can note that someone wanting to learn how to improve public education would want to design a quite different evaluation.

When you try to make sense of evaluations that others have done or are proposing, you may see that parents, teachers, administrators, and policy makers want different things evaluated, even if the different wishes have been lumped together. For example, regarding high-stakes standardized tests, evaluations of the following different things are supposed to come from the one test: students' knowledge; new curricular frameworks as a means to improve students' knowledge; performance of teachers; performance of schools; and performance of school districts. In contrast to this example, you should separate the different kinds of evaluation for any issue you are interested in, and address each evaluation appropriately. More generally, you should add notes from your own critical thinking about what others have done: Why evaluate in this situation? Why this evaluation and not another? What theories are hidden behind the intervention that was implemented? What supports are given to people to make the intervention?

A note on working from newspaper articles: Often a newspaper article will not give you information for every step in the clock. For the missing steps, fill in what you would do in the shoes of someone in the corresponding position, i.e., designing an evaluation (for the early steps), interpreting it (for the middle steps), or deciding on proposals to make (for the later steps). As in **Action Research**, deciding what you would do is a matter of making proposals that follow from research results and presenting the proposals to potential constituencies who might take them up if the research supports them.

FULL CLOCK

0a. The *intervention* whose effect or effectiveness needs to be evaluated is...
("Intervention" here is an umbrella term for an action, a change in a program, policy, curriculum, practice, or treatment, a difference between two situations, etc.)
0b. Interest or concern in the effect/iveness of the intervention arises because...

—
1a. The group or person(s) that sponsor the evaluation of the intervention are...
1b. The people they seek to influence with the results are...
1c. The actions or decisions or policies those people might improve or affirm concern...

2. General Question: The comparison needed to evaluate the effectiveness of the intervention is between two (or more) situations, namely a. a comparison of...

b. with respect to differences in the general area of...…..

3. Specific observables: To undertake that comparison, the effects of the intervention will be assessed by looking at the following specific variable(s) in the two (or more) situations...

4. The methods to be used to produce observations or measurements of those variables are...(survey, questionnaire, etc.)

5a. The people who will be observed or measured are...
5b. The observing or measuring is done in the following places or situations... or derived indirectly from the following sources...

6. The observations or measurements will be analyzed in the following manner to determine whether the two situations are significantly different...

7a. Given that people who will interpret (give meaning to) the analysis are...
7b. the analysis will be summarized/conveyed in the following form...

When the results are available, the following steps can be pinned down. In the design stage, you should lay out different possibilities.
8a. The results show that what has been happening is...
8b. This will be reported through the following outlets...

9. What has been happening is happening because...

10. The lessons learned by sponsors of evaluation are that...

11. What the sponsors should now do differently is...

STRIPPING DOWN THE "CLOCK" TO FOCUS ON THE COMPARISON INVOLVED IN EVALUATING THE EFFECTS OF ANY INTERVENTION

0. The *intervention* whose effect or effectiveness needs to be evaluated is...
("Intervention" here is an umbrella term for an action, a change in a program, policy, curriculum, practice, or treatment, a difference between two situations, etc.)

—

2. The comparison needed to evaluate the effect/iveness of the intervention is between two (or more) situations, namely comparing...

—

3. To undertake that comparison, the effects of the intervention will be assessed by looking at the following specific variable(s) in the two situations...

—

4. The methods to be used to produce observations or measurements of those variables are...(survey, questionnaire, etc.)

—

5. The people who will be observed or measured are...
This is done in the following places or situations... or derived indirectly from the following sources...

5 F's: Find, Focus, Filter, Face Fears, File

Background research involves a continuing interplay among the 5 F's: Find, Focus, Filter, Face Fears, File.

5F's to keep in play as you proceed in your background research

Find: Develop skills in using bibliographic searches, enlisting timely assistance from library personnel, identifying initial guides or informants, and so on. What you Find may relate to what you are Focused on or to material that leads you to refine or rethink that Focus.

Focus: Ask yourself "What am I looking for now? What do I know and what do I need to know to keep moving forward?" Your Focus will evolve as you Filter and **Actively Digest** what you Find.

Filter: You cannot read everything you Find, so check out the article's title, introduction, topic or thesis, ending, and subheadings to see whether and how it connects with your project. If it does not connect with your current Focus, put the article to the side or into the recycle bin. What you do read should be Actively Digested, so you can refine your Focus.

Face Fears: Your ability to Find may be inhibited if you Fear that others have already done what you want to, or if you Fear your work is not important unless it is completely original. If you Face your Fears, you can accept that the work of many others overlaps or intersects with your work. You can even embrace that work, being confident that, in the end, your project will be original because no-one before has ever been weaving that project into *your work and life*.

File: To help you Focus, clear your physical and computer desktops of material you are not using right now. File the printouts and notes in places organized and labeled so you can Find them again easily.

Expect to be fuzzy or unfocused at first, but do not insist on clarifying your Focus before trying to Find material. Instead, start with your initial Focus and let it evolve as you see what material you Find (or do not Find), Filter that material, and Face your Fears. Keep the 5F's (or 6F's depending on how you count Face Fears) in play as your research into **Background Information** proceeds.

(see **Phase B**)

Focused Conversation

In a Focused Conversation a facilitator asks questions to elicit responses that take the group from the surface of a topic to its depth (Stanfield 1997). The four-stage process of a focused conversation disrupts people's tendency to be selective in the data they deem relevant and to jump to premature conclusions based on that selective data (which is the *ladder of inference* problem described by Ross 1994).

Sample Script

(In this sample script an instructor facilitates a Focused Conversation on the early activities in a course that introduces the **Cycles and Epicycles for Action Research** framework. ... refers to omitted details about what has gone on in that particular course.)

You have quite a challenge before you for the rest of the semester... But I think you can be pleasantly surprised by looking at how much you have learned already through...

To do that, I'm going to lead you in a Focused Conversation. This is a series of questions that begin with concrete things you observed and move through feelings and associations, on to interpretations and finally get to the overall implications. The idea is to avoid jumping to conclusions or holding on to preformed opinions. Instead, stay open to forming new conclusions on the basis of hearing everyone's responses to the earlier questions—and this includes your own responses. So try not to answer a question that has not yet been asked.

This Focused Conversation is not a conventional discussion. You do not directly address what someone has said before you, but contribute to a pool of responses and gain insight from listening to what others contribute. We want each person to be heard, so keep your answers to the questions short and pithy—even telegraphic. No speeches and no disputing particular speaker's contributions. Leave it to me to ask for clarification.

I'm not the instructor here, but a neutral facilitator, so do not look to me for endorsement of answers. Instead listen to what others say. As long as you are responding to the question that was asked, there are no wrong answers. There is insight in every answer.

Objective Questions = concrete things, actually observable by all
- What are the main parts of the Action Research process?
- What are useful tools in the Action Research process?

Reflective Questions = associations and feelings
- What was relatively easy for you to do in the initial activities?
- What felt difficult?
- What similar experiences come to mind?

Interpretive Questions = meaning and significance
- What skills and resources did you bring to the initial activities?
- What skills and resources were you missing?
- What issues need to be resolved?

Decisional questions = implications for the future [notes recorded on the board or on a flip chart]
- What tasks do you plan to undertake this week?
- What guidance will you seek?

Closing: I'm always impressed with what emerges when people combine their insights. I'll type up the notes and email them to you by tomorrow.
But for now, let's close this conversation and call it a day.

Freewriting

Freewriting is a technique that helps you clear mental space so that thoughts about an issue in question can emerge that had been below the surface of your attention—insights that you were not able, at first, to acknowledge. (**Supportive Listening** is another means to that end.) Elbow (1981) places Freewriting on the creative side of the necessary interplay of the creative and the critical in thinking and writing. You may wish to make Freewriting a start-of-the-day habit to warm up your research and writing.

In a Freewriting exercise, you should not take your pen off the paper. Keep writing even if you find yourself stating over and over again, "I don't know what to say." What you write will not be seen by anyone else, so do not go back to tidy up sentences, grammar, or spelling. In a *guided* freewriting exercise, you continue from where a sentence provided by the session facilitator leaves off (examples below). You will probably diverge from the topic, at least for a time, while you acknowledge other preoccupations. That is OK—indeed, it is another purpose of the exercise. However, if you keep writing for seven to ten minutes, you should expose some thoughts about the topic that had been below the surface of your attention.

At the start of a project
• "I would like my work on [topic X] to influence [group Y] to make changes in [situation Z]..."
• "I often/sometimes have trouble getting going until..."
• "The differences between investigating ... and investigating... might be that..."
• "There are *so* many aspects to my topic. I could look at... and..."
• "If I were given more background in how to analyze..., I would be better able to..."
• "From my past experience, the kinds of issues or aspects of research I tend to overlook or discount include..."

Early on in a project
- "When I think about sharing my incomplete work, what comes up is... And this means I should....."
- "It may be very premature to lay out the arguments involved in my research, but it may help me define where I am going, so let me try..."
- "Incorporating regular freewriting into my research practice is (difficult? wonderful? a not-yet-achieved ideal?)..."
- "In the next two months what I most want to see happening in my project is... What is blocking me realizing this vision is..."
- "Usually when I try to plan my work, what happens is.."
- "Some aspect of research I would like to be able to explain clearly for my project is..."
- "If I had to state a question that keeps my subject, audience and purpose most clearly in focus, I would say..."

When you begin to draft a report
- "My ideal report would lead readers to see... I would grab their attention by... and lead them through a series of steps, namely..."

Gallery Walk

A Gallery Walk is an ice breaker activity for a group's first meeting. It serves to introduce participants to each other as well as to acknowledge that they already know a lot about the topic at hand, including knowing what they need to learn. The principle here is that, if their knowledge is elicited and affirmed, participants become better at learning from others. Other reasons for the activity are given after the following two examples.

As participants in a course or workshop arrive at the first meeting, they can be grouped in twos or threes, given marker pens, asked to introduce themselves to each other, and directed to one of a number of flip chart stations. Each flip chart has a question. Participants review the answers already contributed by any previous groups, add their own, then move in one direction around the stations.

When the first groups returns to where they began, volunteers from those groups are asked to go to one of the stations and summarize the main themes and the contrasts. They present these summaries to the whole group, with the aid of a single PowerPoint slide, overhead transparency, or photocopied sheet, or by drawing on the flip chart in question. If a sheet listing the questions is distributed to all the participants, everyone can take notes on what is presented.

Example A: Gallery Walk questions for the first class of a course on "Evaluation of Educational Change"
1. What changes (big and small) are being pursued in teaching, schools, and educational policy?
2. What kinds of experience prepare teachers, administrators, and policy makers to pursue change in constructive ways?
3. What things would tell us that positive educational changes had happened?
4. What do you hope will come from this semester's experience?

Example B: Gallery Walk questions used at the start of a year-long professional development course for math and science educators to promote inquiry and problem-solving in a watershed context.
1. What factors (big and small) are involved in maintaining healthy watersheds?
2. What watershed issues might translate well into math. and science teaching?
3. What pressures & challenges do you see facing teachers wanting to improve math. and science teaching?
4. What has helped you in the past make improvements successfully (+), and what has hindered you (-)?
5. What things would tell you that positive educational changes had happened?
6. What kinds of things do you hope will come from this professional development experience?

The following reasons have been given for using the Gallery Walk at the start of a course (STEMTEC 1998). Analogous reasons apply to the start of any group's work together.
1. Breaks the ice and introduces students who might otherwise never interact.
2. Begins the community-building process so central to cooperative learning and emphasizes the collaborative, constructed nature of knowledge.
3. Suggests to students their centrality in the course, and that their voices, ideas, and experiences are significant and valued.
4. Allows for both consensus and debate—two skills essential to knowledge-building—and facilitates discussion when the class reconvenes as a larger group.
5. Enables physical movement around the room, an important metaphor for the activity at the course's core.
6. Depending on the gallery walk questions, provides one way for the instructor to gauge prior knowledge and skills, and identify potentially significant gaps in these.
7. Depending on the gallery walk questions, provides a way to immediately introduce students to a central concept, issue or debate

in the field.

8. Through reporting back, provides some measure of closure by which students can assess their own understandings.

GOSP

A presentation or written report on your project should achieve the following:

Grab the audience's attention.

(It is often helpful for listeners or readers to hear or read something that explains how you personally got involved in this inquiry, or what it means to you; see **Sense-Making** contextualization.)

Orient the audience to
- the direction of your movement in undertaking the project, and
- where your talk or paper will take the audience.

(In the spirit of orienting the audience to what you are working towards, verbs are important. E.g., Instead of a report title such as "Lack of funds for girls' sport," consider "Convincing corporations to fund girls' sport.")

Steps, that is, the overall argument or progression that leads your audience to the

Position you want them at least to appreciate, whether or not they agree with your concluding Propositions.

(see **Phase H**)

Governing Question

The Governing Question specifies what you need to investigate to make progress in your project. (It is not your thesis.) It should be expressed in a way that orients your work. For example:

• "In what ways can approaches for effectively teaching empathy-based personal interaction be combined into a course for employees and managers?"

• "What do I need to know to influence people who prescribe or seeks drugs for behavioral modification of children?"

• "What teachers, theories, organizations, examples can provide models for me to experiment with and make my own so that..."

A clear Governing Question should keep your attention focused on what you need to find out that you do not already know or that you cannot yet demonstrate to someone else. The question should be grounded in what *you* need to know to get engaged in your specific circumstances, not what some generic person ought to know. Keeping the Governing Question in mind as you do research will help guide you through the complexity of possible considerations so that you more easily prioritise what you read, whom you speak to, and, in general, what you do in your project.

Any gap between the Governing Question and the **Paragraph Overview** probably points to unresolved issues about your subject, purpose, and audience. You should not leave it for your advisor or other readers to point this out. To see the gap for yourself, put the Governing Question at the top of your first page of what you write —whether at your project's early stages, such as in an **Annotated Bibliography**, or later when you prepare a **Drafts**. Having the Governing Question as a banner helps remind you to check that what you are writing sticks to what you intended or claimed to be writing about. If the Governing Question and what you are writing do not match, something has to be re-envisioned.

(see **Phase A**)

Historical Scan

A Historical Scan is used either to review a group's evolution over time or to set the scene in which a project is to be undertaken. It is a variant of the **Focused Conversation** (Stanfield 1997), so let us review that process first:

Focused Conversation
A group (which could be students in a course, a grass roots activist organization, or a business) addresses some challenging or difficult situation by proceeding through four stages:

1. Objective (getting the facts)
2. Reflective (eliciting feelings and associations)
3. Interpretive (considering the meaning and significance)
4. Decisional (formulating a decision, an action, or a shared picture)

Participants who tend to jump quickly to a decision or an interpretation are encouraged, instead, to spend more time on the earlier stages, to be careful to separate facts from feelings, and to recognize at each step the range of assessments put forward by all the participants. The result of a Focused Conversation is not necessarily a consensus. Yet, because the group shares a common pool of experiences of the situation, the result is larger than what any one person had beforehand. There is a firmer basis for the group's work to be extended, either by the group or by group members in other settings.

In a Historical Scan, as in a Focused Conversation, the facilitator should, as neutrally as possible, lead the group through a series of questions. Answers should be telegraphic, so as to allow for as wide a pool of contributions as possible. To give the four-step process a chance to have its effect, participants should try to answer the question asked and not jump ahead to give their overall conclusion, even if others have.

Sample scripts

At the end of a group project or course
"As this project (course) draws to a close, let's look back at the

experiences we've had, from the time you heard of this project (course) on *[insert project (course) topic]* until today.

Take a moment to jot down specific concrete things that struck you, e.g., *[insert range of examples]*,....

Now choose five* of them and write them in on the large Post-its in as large block letters as will fit. *[* Adjust this number to ensure 40-60 Post-its for the group as a whole.]*

Select one from early on in the period. *[Put them on the board, consulting the group to keep them in order]*

... from the middle... from the later part of the project (course)... others *[including those covering the whole period]*

When were you excited?... discouraged?

What do these experiences remind you of?

When were there transitions?

If this were a book, what name would you give for the "chapters" between the transitions?

...name for the whole "book"?

What have you learned about a diverse group of people coming together to "read this book"? *[Remind participants to be telegraphic —no speeches.]*

What have you learned about facilitating planning, or action, or thinking and learning as they relate to *[insert project (course) topic]*?

How shall you translate the learning to future situations?"

When setting the scene in which a project is to be undertaken
"As you consider your involvement in this project, let's paint a picture of the context in which we will be operating. Let's think about this context having a past and a possible future and operating on three levels: *local, regional,* and *global [see note below].*

Take a moment to jot down significant events at each of the levels over the past xx years or a future event that you hope will be in the yy years ahead.

[Then continue as in the script above, replacing "events" for "experiences" and "what you will do in the project" for future situations."]

Note: As described in Tuecke [2000], the *global* is the largest view relevant to the project, which may be the world, but may also be the profession. The *local* is the personal perspective gained in the immediate unit (family, workplace, etc.). The *regional* is the specific arena in which the project operates, e.g., the management of water resources (in an environmental context) or the state educational system (in the context of improving school outcomes).

Initial Guide

Identify and talk with someone who can guide your inquiries in their initial unformed stage by providing you with leads to key people to read and contact. You do this so as to avoid finding out late in the project that there was a key person or article that you should have known about weeks before.

You may notice a tendency to procrastinate on making contact with an Initial Guide. Perhaps this is related to a feeling that other people's work threatens your originality. This feeling is not helpful —part of developing your own approach is to connect with others in your area. Therefore, make contact with possible Initial Guides and make an appointment for a meeting early on in the project, preferably before session 4. Afterwards, reflect on what you learned by preparing a brief verbal report to give when you next meet with your advisor or peers.

Note: Making contact with an initial guide is different from interviewing someone. Interviewing makes sense later, under **Phase F**.

(see **Phase B**)

Interview Guide

An interview guide ensures that you set the scene clearly, do not forget essential things at the start and end, and can refer to a checklist of items you wanted to cover. Having a guide helps you relax and participate in a smoothly flowing verbal exchange. (*Smoothly flowing*, not *natural*, because one person asking another a series of questions is not a natural form of conversation.) What follows is an abbreviated example of an Interview Guide.

Sample guide

Introductory comments
As I mentioned by email, I've read your book on bungee jumping, but today I'd like to hear about your experiences taking the first steps (so to speak) as a bungee jumping instructor and how you went from there to end up running a whole school.

But first, there are some preliminaries:
- We have 40 minutes, right? Is that still OK with you?
- Can I record this so I'm not distracted by note taking?
- What kinds of restrictions do you want to place on my use of the recording?

A journalist-style release form might specify the options for the interviewee to choose amongst, then sign and date.
a. No restrictions
b. If a transcript of the recording is made, I wish to read the transcript and make corrections and emendations.
c. My permission is required to quote or reproduce from the recording or corrected transcript (if applicable).
d. Only if my paper is subsequently to be submitted for publication or used in the preparation of any manuscript intended for publication do I need to be consulted, in which case a new release form governing the use of the material must be provided and signed by me.
e. Only if other scholars want access to the recording or corrected transcript (if applicable) do I need to be consulted, in which case a new release form governing the use of the material must be provided and signed by me.
This constitutes our entire and complete understanding.

Do you have a resume or c.v. that I can get from you before I leave so I don't need to interrupt our conversation to check on those kind of details?

OK. Let's get going.

When did you start teaching bungee jumping? What had you been doing before then?

[Beginning an interview this way allows the interviewee to tell a chronological story of their process starting with the time of transition into the area of interest to you. You can ask for more details at any point or take them back to something that they skipped over, then continue the story where you had broken in. The story format works against your being fed the take-home lessons when you actually want to know about the process, including how the interviewees picked themselves up when down or got back on track when they had taken an unproductive turn. Sometimes the experience of being interviewed is valuable to the interviewees because they find themselves making sense of what they have done. Having both the interviewer and interviewee benefit is the ideal outcome.

If a chronological format is not appropriate for your interview, make sure the order of questions allows the interviewee to build on previous answers and feel that they are making sense of their experience, not simply replying to what seems to be a scatter-shot of questions. (The order of the **Sense-Making** contextualization is helpful for developing a logical sequence to the questions.)]

Can I take a moment to review my notes and see if there are issues we haven't covered?....

[Here you refer to the items you have listed on your guide.]

Looking back on the whole process of your personal and professional development, what lessons would you draw?

Are there other key people you think I should talk with?

Is then anything I didn't ask you about that I should have asked about?

Much thanks for making the time to speak with me. Can I get a copy of that resume before I go?

(see **Phase F**)

Jigsaw Discussion of Texts

The Jigsaw Discussion method allows all members of a group to get up to steam on issues raised by a set of readings without everyone having read every reading (or document) in depth. If there are R readings and N people in the whole group, each reading should be assigned to X = N/R people to read it in depth. (The activity works better, of course, if people read more than the one reading assigned to them.)

Instructions to Participants

Preparation

As you read, identify items to highlight when you talk with someone who has not concentrated on that reading. You want to be able to help them appreciate the significance of the case study, theory, or conclusions presented in the reading. Items to highlight may include questions or issues that you think need clarification or debate.

In the group meeting (or class)

The readings will be discussed in two steps:

1. *Common discussion:* In sub-groups of X people who concentrated on the same reading, discuss the article. Identify the key points and the issues you need clarified. Each person prepares a sheet of notes to use during step 2. (If X > 5, break into groups of 2-4 people.)

2. *Cross-cutting discussion:* In sub-groups of R people who read different readings, describe the key points and the issues that your common discussion sub-group wanted clarified or subject to debate.

The discussion in groups may follow the **Small-Group Roles**, with roles merged to match the number of people in the sub-group.

Variant of the Instructions

Choose for yourself which of the readings to read. The sub-groups for the common and cross-cutting discussions in steps 1 and 2 above may be of different size and not every reading will end up covered by every cross-cutting sub-group. If you are the only person to have concentrated on a particular reading, instead of participating in a common discussion for step 1, you join a cross-cutting discussion sub-group with any others in the same singleton boat as you.

KAQF

The KAQF framework helps you organize your thinking and research keeping an eye on *actions*, that is, what you might do or propose or plan on the basis of the results.

KAQF chart

What do I **K**now? (or claim to know)
(Q: How do I Know that?—What is the evidence, assumptions, and reasoning?)

Action: What actions could people pursue on the basis of accepting this knowledge?
(Q: Which people or group?)

Questions for inquiry: What more do I Need to know—in order to clarify what people could do (A) or to revise/refine/support the knowledge claim (K)

How to **F**ind this out? (Methods, Steps..)
(Q: What alternatives methods are possible for inquiring into this Question? Will my method of research best enable me to Find this out?)

Make a template of this chart so you can copy it each time you start a new set of KAQF's.

For each KAQF chart start with a Knowledge claim *OR* with a proposed Action *OR* with a Question for inquiry you wish to consider. Then fill in the rest of the KAQF's that connects with that starting point. For example, if you entered a proposed Action, then write down what Knowledge claim(s) this Action is based on. Then move forward to identify Questions for inquiry that follow and how you might Find out the answer to the Question.

In Problem-based learning (PBL), the Actions should address the objective stated in the PBL scenario (see Snapshot 7 in Part 4's Teaching and Learning for Reflective Practice). In **Action Research**, the Actions should be related to the problem(s) behind your Action Research, including developing a constituency to act on any findings or proposals you come up with. Of course, research and thinking will often modify your ideas about the problem and appropriate actions, especially when, as you start the Action Research cycle, you **Evaluate** the effects of past actions (or learn about the evaluations others have done) and inquire more broadly so as to fill in relevant background.

The additional questions in parentheses in the KAQF chart are included to check your thinking. (Asking another person to be your sounding board also helps in this matter.) E.g., In PBL, how is the research you are formulating related to the objective specified by the PBL scenario? In Action Research, is the research you are formulating related to the problem(s) behind your Action Research? In either situation, if the connection is not clear, go back and revise the entries in your chart.

When you have completed all four items—the K, the A, the Q, and the F—as well as you can for *one* starting point, draw a line underneath this and start another KAQF chart. Do not mix KAQFs from different starting points into one omnibus sequence —That does not help you keep clear how a specific K matches a specific A matches a Q matches an F.

As additional Knowledge claims, Action proposals, or Questions for inquiry occur to you, start another KAQF chart. (Additional K's, A's, or Q's may emerge from checking your thinking on the previous KAQF charts.)

After you have many KAQF charts, prioritize the research you need to do (that is, your F's) and start that research—or plan how you would do it.

Key Article

An article or book chapter is key for your project if it provides many references to other publications. A review article or an examination of a relevant controversy can fit the bill well. An article is not key simply because it affirms your gut feelings about the topic or gives you entry points for research. The goal is to find a publication that moves you well towards being able to say: "I know what others have done before that informs and connects with my project."

(see **Phase B**)

Making Space for Taking Initiative In and Through Relationships

This process has several layers. In order to pursue the **Reflective Practitioner Goals** you have to take initiative. In particular, you have to take initiative in relationships, such as those with your advisors and peers. At the same time, it is *through* the relationships you develop as you pursue these goals—including your relationship with yourself—that you find support for the risk-taking and change that is involved in taking initiative *in* relationships. Yet, not all the reflective practitioner goals pull you in the same direction; or, at least, it is difficult to attend to them all simultaneously. You might focus on a few at any given time, but the challenge is to keep the other considerations in mind and address any tensions among them. All these layers, but especially the last challenge, are what it means to make space for taking initiative in and through relationships.

The schema below identifies six aspects of this process: negotiating power and standards (a "vertical" relationship); building peer (or "horizontal") relationships; exploring differences and diversity among people); acknowledging that affect (i.e., emotion) is involved in what you are doing and not doing (and in how others respond to that); developing autonomy (so that you are neither too sensitive nor impervious to feedback); and clearing away distractions from other sources (present and past) so you can "be here now." Do not expect to learn or change without moving among or being *jostled* by the interplay or tensions between these different considerations. For example, to "be here now" might involve shaping relationships so that others can and want to help you by taking over responsibility of things that have been distracting you.

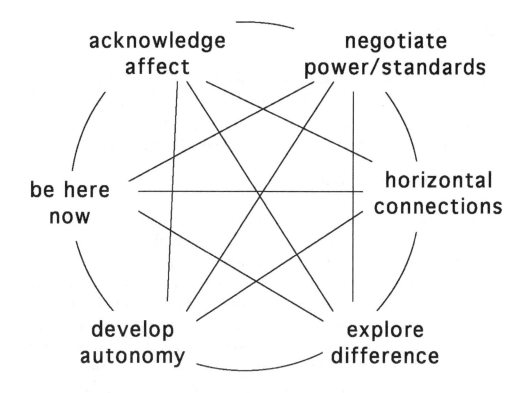

Six aspects of making space for taking initiative in and through relationships

Mapping

The goal of Mapping is the same as for **Phase C**, namely, to expose possible new directions and clarify direction and scope within the larger set of issues. The idea is to do mapping *before* you have a coherent overall **Research Design** and **Overall Argument**.

Step 1 (opening wide)

Start in the center of a large sheet of paper stating the issue that concerns *you*. You may want to know more about it, advocate a change, design a curriculum unit or a workshop, and so on.

Draw connections from that issue to related considerations and other issues. (Post-its are useful, so you can move things around.)

To tease out connections, you might want to start with a dump-sheet or stack of Post-its in which you address the **Questions for Opening Wide and for Probing**. Alternatively, you may simply allow yourself to brainstorm (i.e., put down everything that comes to mind without stopping to consider its relevance).

Step 2 (opening wide and beginning to focus in)

Color coding or symbols you invent will allow you to take note of patterns in the connections and their significance to you. You may even rearrange the connections and redraw the map. After doing that, explain the map to someone else, inviting them to do the following:

• Ask questions with a view to getting clear about your issue, who you want to reach, and what would be involved in influencing that audience (see **Phase A**), and

• *Probe* with the same set of Probing Questions.

The interaction between the mapper and the questioner(s) should expose many additional questions that warrant research (or sub-projects), force greater clarity in definitions of terms and categories, and help you see how to frame your inquiries in a way that satisfies your interests yet does not expand out of control.

Step 3 (focus in and formulate)

Out of the preceding interaction you should eventually see an aspect of the map's complexity that engages you most. Or, to introduce another image, you should look for a path on which you can move through the complexity while turning to the side from time to time so you do not lose sight of the wider terrain. You should also be able to define or refine the **Governing Question** that conveys what you need to research (and what you no longer need to research). For example, for a map of research on the color of hospital rooms, the question might be: "What research needs to be done to convince hospital designers and administrators that room color is one of the environmental features that can contribute to patient healing?" Using **Freewriting** after mapping may help you define such a question for yourself.

Models from the Past

At the start of a research and writing process, review previous reports to get a sense of the scope of previous projects and the look of the final products. Make notes and digest what you are reviewing: "This interests me," or conversely: "This is not my cup of tea." You can then ask: "What is it that they have done?" (e.g., inserted real cases, not given enough reference to solid research, used too much text without illustrations). Through this process you can begin to define your own direction.

(see **Phase A**)

Narrative Outline

A Narrative Outline or plan of your report has explanatory sentences inserted at key places:
• to explain in a declarative style the point of each section; and
• to explain how each section links to the previous one and to the larger section or the whole report it is part of.

Three steps may be needed to arrive at such an outline. First, prepare a standard outline, i.e., one that looks like a table of contents. Then turn it into a *nested and connected table of contents* as follows:
• nest or indent subsections inside sections, and sub-subsections inside subsections; and
• indicate with arrows and annotations how each section or subsection connects with the previous one, and how each connects with the larger whole (including the report) of which it is a part.
Finally, insert the explanatory sentences mentioned above.

Insertion of the explanatory sentences helps you move beyond the preliminary thinking that goes into a standard outline. For *some* people a standard outline has *some* value. However, for most writers it does not ensure that, when you write, your ideas and material really will fit your outline and the draft will flow from your "pen" (keyboard). This fit and flow is more likely if you have prepared a Narrative Outline.

(See **Phase G**)

One-on-one Session

As a researcher and writer, you meet with an advisor to discuss progress, plans, concerns, and questions. One-on-one Sessions should begin early in the project and be scheduled to allow timely resolution of any misunderstandings about the advisor's comments on written work and your responses to them. Discussions about misunderstandings often provide a chance to open up significant issues about your relationship to audience and influencing others.

When one-on-one sessions are free-form, which is typically the case, advisors are free to offer advice that may or may not be what you were looking for right then. It can be fruitful instead to give sessions a more mindful structure. For example, a 30-minute meeting can be divided into three phases:

First 1/4: Researcher and advisor **Freewrite** to take stock of where things are at and identify their goals and priorities for the discussion.

Middle 1/2: Discussion that follows the researcher's goals and priorities first. Time permitting, additional issues are introduced by the advisor.

Final 1/4: Researcher and advisor separately make notes of what they learned from the discussion.

One-on-one Consultations within a Group

This activity ("Office Hours" for short) provides opportunities for group members to solicit specific advice one on one. It can also be enlightening to see who asks you for advice and what you find yourself able to say. The activity can be slotted one or more times into a meeting or workshop when there is 45-60 minutes to spare.

Instructions about Signing Up

[Before circulating this sign-up sheet, the coordinator of this activity fills in the left-hand column with the names of all participants.]
• You can sign up to consult with other people by putting your name on their line for a time slot that is *empty for both of you*. Then put a cross on your own line for that time slot (which prevents someone signing up to consult with you at a time when you would be meeting with someone else.)
• You may sign up for one or two consultations, but, before you sign up for a third consult, give everyone else a chance to sign up at least once.
• If you want to sign up to consult with a person who is already signed up to consult with you, sign up in a separate time slot for a consult with them. (That ensures that both of you have the chance to set your own agenda for a full time slot.)

Person to be consulted (below)	Time Slot 1	Time Slot 2	Time Slot 3

(Add lines as needed)

Additional Instructions

- If any two people are not signed up for a given time slot, the coordinator should pair them up and they will split the time in mutual support (possibly following **Supportive Listening** guidelines).
- If there is an odd number of people, the coordinator should ask for one of the pairs to become a triad.
- Pairs of chairs need to be set up and spaced widely to minimize distractions from other conversations. At the start of the time slot, find the person you signed up to consult with and move to a pair of chairs. Then start consulting!

Overall Argument— Clarification

To clarify the Overall Argument of the project is to identify the *steps* or progression that leads your audience to the *position* you want them at least to appreciate, whether or not they agree with it. In other words, the Overall Argument is the S and P of **GOSP**. It serves as a skeleton that gives shape and structure to the body of your report. The use of the word "argument" does not mean there must be a dispute you are having with someone else.

Note: The Overall Argument is distinct from the various **Component Propositions** and premises that your project depends on.

(see **Phase G**)

Paragraph Overview

In a single prose paragraph you can *orient* potential readers to your project if you convey where you are going in three senses:
• the broad steps in your investigation;
• the knowledge or shift of perspective you want to lead your intended audience towards; and
• biographical or background information that makes you want to address the issue. (Your topic may seem worthy, but what makes *you* a person to address it?)

In orienting readers, you are also articulating your audience, subject, and purpose: Who you want to reach? What you want to convey to them? Why do *you* want to address them about that? In orienting readers, you are also orienting yourself as you move along in your project. In that spirit, your **Governing Question** should be woven into the paragraph or even lead it off. Both the Governing Question and the Paragraph Overview should be revised as soon as you see that your direction is shifting.

The idea of limiting this to a *single prose* paragraph is that, if you write more than one paragraph or use bullet points, it is harder for you and your readers to see whether the audience, subject, and purpose hang together well.

(see **Phase A**)

Personal and Professional Development Workbook

In a Personal and Professional Development (PPD) Workbook you assemble and organize installments of your project, comments you receive on them, and various other items that emerge during your research. Having a PPD workbook allows you to readily pick up after a break what you were thinking and to see emerging patterns that warrant your attention. In the same way that keeping a portfolio of your work helps an advisor make generative comments (see **Dialogue Around Written Work**), having your own PPD Workbook helps you to bring to the surface, form, and articulate your ideas as a researcher.

One way to think about what to include in a PPD Workbook and how to organize it is to imagine returning to the material a year or more later. What items, annotations, and organization would make it possible to quickly re-engage with your own thinking and processes of development? You might prefer to assemble these materials mostly on your computer or online on a wiki. Typically, however, you will have some paper as well as computer files and you will need cross-references from one medium to the other.

The items in the PPD Workbooks might include:
• Notes on readings and other preparation for each **Phase** or part of the **Cycles and Epicycles of Action Research** process
• Notes and printouts from activities during the sessions
• Installments, comments from readers, and revisions, which document Dialogue Around Written Work
• Weekly journal-like reflections that explore the relationship between, on one hand, your interests and project, and, on the other hand, the readings, activities, and tools introduced during the sessions
• Annotated clippings from print and internet sources (to keep up with current developments and to develop good habits for life-long

learning)

- **Self-Assessment at Mid-Project** (including a report on the gap between where you are and where you would like to be in relation to your **Research Organization**—both on paper and on your computer—and research and study competencies (CCT 2010)
- **Process Review** at the end of the project

Plus-Delta Feedback

Feedback that begins with an appreciation (*plus* or +) makes any subsequent suggestion for change (*delta* or Δ) more likely to be heard and taken up. It also has an effect on our giving of such feedback, namely, to shift us away from being consumers or critics and make us collaborators or supporters of the ongoing development of the recipient of our feedback.

Plus-Delta Feedback can be given verbally and quickly—thus more regularly—at the end of sessions in a go-around or **Closing Circle** (Check-Out) in which each person contributes only one + item and one Δ item.

Plus-Delta Feedback can also be used for self-evaluation. For this you need a set of objectives and for each you state a plus (something you did well) and a delta (some way to improve or develop).

Process Review

In a Process Review at the end of a project (or course), you identify four to six examples or exhibits that capture the process of development of your work and your thinking about the subject of the project (or course). The examples chosen need not be your best work—you might include entries from your **PPD workbook**, **Freewriting**, drafts of submissions, and so on. You explain your choices in a one or two page cover note for the whole Process Review and in annotations of each individual example or exhibit.

(see **Phase J**)

Pyramid of Questions

A Pyramid of Questions is a compilation of all the questions that arise as your project proceeds. (The term *pyramid* is used because later questions build on earlier ones). In order to review the Pyramid as a whole from time to time, you should compile it in a part of your notebook or **PPD workbook** separate from the **Freewriting**, personal reflections, and other notes. In the Pyramid include the initial questions—general and specific—for your projects, successive variants of your **Governing Question**, questions that arise during research on **Background Information**, possible questions to ask **Initial Guides**, questions needing research that emerge through **Mapping** and teasing out of **Component Propositions**, and so on. These questions could be crossed out when no longer central to your evolving project, checked when satisfactorily addressed, and asterisked when given high priority.

(see **Phase C**)

Questions for Opening Wide and for Probing

At the center of your **Map** should be an issue that concerns you in the sense that you may want to know more about it, advocate a change, design a curriculum unit or a workshop, and so on. The following questions allow you to tease out considerations that are connected to this issue.

- Where is this an issue—where is the controversy happening?
- Who are the different groups implicated?
- What changes could be promoted?
- What are arguments for change for the change and counter-arguments.
- What categories of things (and sub-categories) are involved in your subject?
- What definitions are involved?
- What related questions have other people investigated?
- Where is there a need for primary versus secondary research?
- What is the general area and what are specific questions?
- What are the background versus focal issues?
- What is your provisional proposal?
- What are the research holes that need to be filled?
- What would you be able to do with that additional knowledge?
- What ambiguity emerges in all this—what are tensions and oppositions?

(see **Phase C**)

Reflective Practitioner Goals

Developing as a reflective practitioner overlaps substantially with **Making Space for Taking Initiative In and Through Relationships**. In addressing the goals to follow readers who are not students should substitute "research and writing projects" for references to "courses" and "programs of study." The **Plus-Delta** format is suitable for taking stock of these goals as the project proceeds and in a **Self-Assessment at the End**.

Goals

1. "I have integrated knowledge and perspectives from my current and past courses into my own inquiry and engagement in social or educational change."

2. "I have also integrated into my own inquiry and engagement the processes, experiences, and struggles of previous courses."

3. "I have developed efficient ways to organize my time, research materials, computer access, bibliographies, etc."

4. "I have experimented with new tools and experiences, even if not every one became part of my toolkit as a learner, teacher-facilitator of others, and reflective practitioner."

5. "I have paid attention to the emotional dimensions of undertaking my own project but have found ways to clear away distractions from other sources (present and past) and not get blocked, turning apparent obstacles into opportunities to move into unfamiliar or uncomfortable territory."

6. "I have developed peer and other horizontal relationships. I have sought support and advice from peers, and have given support and advice to them when asked for."

7. "I have taken the lead, not dragged my feet, in dialogue with my advisor and other readers. I did not wait for the them to tell me how to solve an expository problem, what must be read and covered in a literature review, or what was meant by some comment I did not understand. I did not put off giving my writing to my advisor and other readers or avoid talking to them because I thought that they did not see things the same way as I do."

8. "I have revised seriously, which involved responding to the comments of others. I came to see this not as bowing down to the views of others, but taking them in and working them into my own reflective inquiry until I could convey more powerfully to others what I'm about (which may have changed as a result of the reflective inquiry)."

9. "I have inquired and negotiated about formal standards, but gone on to develop and internalize my own criteria for doing work —criteria other than jumping through hoops set by the professor so I get a good grade."

10. "I have approached this course and the program of studies as a whole as works-in-progress, which means that, instead of harboring criticisms to submit after the fact, I have found opportunities to affirm what is working well in the course or program and to suggest directions for their further development."

(see **Phase J**)

Research and Engagement Design

A Research and Engagement Design should emerge from your reflection on the following questions:
• What do you most want to see happening in your project in the time until it has to be submitted?
("Happening" refers both to process and content. It includes, but should not be limited by, who you might be able to influence and what you hope to influence them to do, i.e., your audience and purpose. Take note of your title and evolving **Governing Question**. Do they match each other? Do they dictate what you actually have to do? Revise them if needed.)
• What things might be blocking you from realizing this vision?
• What can you do to deal with the obstacles and realize the vision —what new directions do you need to move in?
• What achievable steps would move you in these directions?
You will have already addressed these questions if you completed the whole **Strategic Personal Planning** process. If you have only done the practical vision stage of Strategic Personal Planning, you will need to use other processes of reflection and dialogue (e.g., **Freewriting**, **One-on-one Session** with advisor) to explore the questions.

In the Design restate your title and Governing Question. The rest of the design may be in note form provided you make evident to readers and to yourself the reasons for the sequence of steps you include.

Sequence of Steps

Map out your research onto the weeks ahead—be more specific about the immediate future. Check whether the steps you propose allow you to fulfill your purpose, answer your Governing Question, and complete research that addresses the **Component Propositions**. Check whether the sequence ensures that when you get to any step you will have completed the preparation necessary for you to undertake that step.

(see **Phase E**)

Research Organization

Principles

1. You do not have enough time in my busy life to have trouble finding a note, a piece of paper, an email, a computer file, an idea —or to spend time recreating them when they are lost. In other words, nobody has time *not* to be organized!

2. Do a favor to yourself-in-the-future. (Analogy: It feels better to come home after a day's work and not find dirty dishes that you left in the sink that morning.)

Tips

1. Carry a notebook with you at all times. Use the book—not pieces of paper—to write notes on. Number the pages and make a table of contents so you can locate these notes later. If you do much of your work on a computer, still carry a notebook for **Freewriting**, thoughts, and leads that arise away from the computer. If you find it hard to make space for reflection you should stay, say, ten minutes after any session or meeting with an advisor to write while your thoughts are fresh.

2. Keep your ears and eyes open to good ideas, but customize the development of your Research Organization to your own situation and foibles. To this end, use a *worksheet* based on the table below to take stock of your research organization and report on it to get feedback from your advisor and others:

a. Spend some time to fill in (or update) the table below, then mark with a * five new things that you plan to implement in the next five weeks. (Making a longer "to do" list makes it more likely that no one thing gets addressed conscientiously.)

	Organization	
	of materials on paper.........	of computer files & records...........
Things that I do that are good (+) or that I avoid as inefficient (-) . . .		
Suggestions of others about good (+) and inefficient (-) practices . . .		

b. Append the following information when you ask for feedback from your advisor on your Research Organization:
• Organization of your computer files. (Be as specific as possible in listing the directory or folder structure you are using.)
• Organization of your paper files. (Be as specific as possible in listing the sections you are dividing your material into and how you are using any other notebook or **Personal and Professional Development Workbook**.)

Reverse Outlining

When you have a draft report that does not **GOSP** readers well, it is worth the time and concentrated effort to do Reverse Outlining. The first step is to work systematically through your draft report, paragraph by paragraph, writing down the topic(s) or claim(s) of each paragraph. Then put the draft to the side and examine the list of topics on its own. Consider how the topics could be rearranged, streamlined, discarded, combined, split, so that the resulting paragraphs would each have a single, unified topic. The topic of each paragraph should, moreover, follow from the previous paragraph's topic and make a distinct contribution to the topic of the section as a whole.

In a similar fashion, you may also need to revise or refine the topic of the sections so that a definite GOSP-ing path is evident in the sequence of topics as they contribute to the topic of the report as a whole. If you skipped the **Narrative Outline** for your report, you should consider going back and doing this before or after the Reverse Outlining.

(see **Phase H**)

Revision

Writing is an essential part of working out your ideas. You do not really understand something until you are able to convey it to someone else. Moreover, you should not expect to work out your ideas in one attempt—everyone needs to revise!

In the first draft of a report or paper or in your preparatory notes you are inventing the problem and delineating the main points. You are getting your thoughts out so as to arrive at a working set of words. Once you have this much of a paper you can (re)organize those points, and after (re)writing the paper you can better identify the weaknesses in it.

Revision begins with a commitment to do more than make cosmetic changes in wording and fine-tuning your word use. You need to allow yourself to *re-envision* the paper. How well does each paragraph connect with the previous one and to the paper as a whole? If the answer is not very well, does the paper need major restructuring? Try shifting sections around; incorporate new insights as they arise. Also ask yourself: Is what I have written true? Have I written about what I set out to write? If not, why not? Have I changed my mind? Re-envisioning requires some distance from your draft. Spend some hours or a day away from it, nominally doing something else but remaining preoccupied with your paper, letting it digest. Whenever and wherever the ideas come to you jot down notes so you can try them out when you return to your writing table.

Next, *fill the holes*. What transitions and links are weak or missing? (Words such as "surely," "it seems," "logically," and so on are common signs of connections that have *not* been made.) Long sentences with many loosely linked ideas are cues that you need to divide the sentence and develop each idea separately. What are your blind spots? Are you avoiding admitting to yourself that you need to do more research? Think about the holes in your information and your argument: Can you fill them? Have you provided examples? Have you anticipated counter-arguments?

Perhaps you feel that you know the meaning of what you have written and there is nothing to change. If so, then read it to others (see Elbow and Belanoff 2000). Do they follow what you mean? Frustratingly, they may not. You may even feel they are being thick or difficult in not understanding you. Perhaps they are. Nevertheless, if you clarify your writing so that thick or difficult readers can follow it, you will probably improve the reading experience for others who could already understand you.

Revision should be proactive. Do not wait for your advisors to slog their way through a rough draft and identify expository problems for you. To be proactive, ask yourself before starting each sentence, paragraph or section: What am I trying to say? What words or phrases express that idea best? After writing a paragraph or section, look back to check that it is about what you said it would be about.

Take responsibility for what you are saying. Check whether you are using a passive construction to avoid getting clear about what group or person your statement actually refers to. (The issue here is not to avoid the passive voice, which is useful for variety and can be less awkward at times. The issue is not to use it to avoid thinking through an issue.)

You should also be prepared to *delete* as well as to add. It may be difficult to overcome your investment in what you have already written, but deletion is an important part of revision.

The aim of writing is not to explain everything for all time, but to achieve some temporary closure. If you cannot fill a hole at this point in time, make clear those places where you—or the field in general—need to do further work. In a few weeks or months you may know more, but the appropriate standard is whether you have finished with the paper for the moment.

After such self-scrutiny and revision you should know pretty well what it is you want to say. *Fine-tuning of vocabulary* to achieve the desired connotations should then be much easier. Watch out for gobbledegook and jargon. Clean this out as much as possible and use plain English.

Finally, even when typing the final draft you should be thinking and not merely transcribing, remaining open to opportunities to rewrite and even restructure your paper so you are saying what you want to as well as you can.

Self-Assessment, Mid-Project

This form of **Taking Stock** at the mid-point of your project (or mid-semester) not only feeds back into the remainder of your work but also contributes to your advisor (instructor) taking stock of how you are learning. This, in turn, feeds back into their advising (teaching) and their future learning about how advisees (students) learn. Submit a copy to the advisor and keep the original for yourself.

NAME:

1. This is what I like about what I have done so far.

2. This is what I plan to do differently from now on.

3. The most difficult thing for me to do is... and so I need support of the following kind...

4. I need more help from my peers on... and from my advisor on...

5. Other comments on the process to date—what you have appreciated and what could be improved?

(see **Phase J**)

Self-Assessment, at the End

For each of a set of goals specified at the start of a project (e.g., the goals that define the **Phases** and the **Reflective Practitioner Goals**), in the **Plus-Delta** mode of taking stock, describe two things:
• one that reflects what you have achieved well related to this goal, and
• one you have struggled with or need more help on or want to work further on.

You may have many examples for some items, but, for a self-assessment to inform the planning and conduct of your future projects, one example is enough. To make use of the self-assessment at a later date, it may help if, after you have written something for all the items, you mark each goal according to a scheme such as the following:

    ** [two stars = "fulfilled very well"],
    * [one star = "did a reasonable job, but room for more development"], or
    - [minus sign = "to be honest, this still needs serious attention"]

Share the Self-Assessment and the markups with your advisor(s). If there are big discrepancies between their assessment and your Self-Assessment, you should discuss the discrepancies and try to come to a shared understanding so as, again, to inform the planning and conduct of your future projects.

Sense-Making Response

This is an approach to **Active Digestion** of what you are reading that involves making notes under each of the following headings:
a) I appreciated...
b) I learned...
c) I wanted to know more about...
d) I struggled with...
e) I would have been helped by...
f) My project connects with this in the following way(s)...
g) I disagreed with...
h) I think the author or presenter should consider...

This form of response to readings takes time and so is not recommended for every article you read. However, the insight gained—the sense you make—by using the Sense-Making response at least once early on in your project can be well worth the time and thought you put in.

Sense-Making Contextualization

Brenda Dervin has developed a "Sense-Making" approach to the development of information seeking and use. One finding from Sense-Making research is that people make much better sense of seminar presentations and other scholarly contributions when these are accompanied by the contextual information in the items below.

Author(s)
Title of paper
a) The essence of the project is...
b) The reason(s) I took this road is (are)...
c) The best of what I have achieved is...
d) What has been particularly helpful to me in this project has been...
e) What has hindered me has been...

f) What I am struggling with is...
g) What would help me now is...

Dervin's Sense-Making approach also leads to recommendations about forms of response that authors and presenters learn most from. By extension, researchers can use similar forms of response to get the most from what they read or listen to, thus the Sense-Making response proposed above.

(see **Phase B**)

Sense of Place Map

A Sense of Place Map is a picture in whatever form occurs to you that addresses three questions:
- Where am I?
- Where have I come from?
- Where am I going?

Although text is not prohibited in a Sense of Place Map, the shift of emphasis from verbal or textual reporting to pictorial representation allows new insights to arise or be brought to the surface. This is akin to the effect of **Freewriting**. As in Freewriting, there should be no obligation to share or display your Map. However, discussion of the typically diverse aspirations and trajectories of group members that emerged through this exercise can be thought-provoking.

A Sense of Place Map may be drawn at the start of a project to provide an impressionistic picture of your aspirations. Or the Map may be drawn at the end of the project to place the project into a longer trajectory of your work and life. These uses of a Sense of Place Map evolved from a more ecological version in Thomashow (1995).

(see **Phase J**)

Sharing of Work to Elicit Responses

Sharing runs through the entire process of research and writing. At one level, sharing might mean simply that you let (or are required to let) others read your work in progress or listen to your spoken thoughts. However, in an evocative passage Elbow (1980, p. 20-21) conveys a deeper sense:

> The essential human act at the heart of writing is the act of *giving*. There's something implacable and irreducible about it: handing something to someone because you want her to have it; not asking for anything in return; and if it is gift of yourself... risking that she won't like it or even accept it. Yet though giving can sound rare and special.., it is of course just a natural and spontaneous human impulse.
>
> This central act of giving is curiously neglected in most writing instruction. Otherwise people would have shared their writing—just given it to another human being for the sake of mutual pleasure—as often as they gave it to a teacher for evaluation and advice. For most people, however, the experience of just sharing what they have written is rare...

To cite Elbow's passage is not to discount the need for feedback and advice. It is simply to suggest that responses can be elicited and offered from a place of mutual respect—and self-respect—for the person doing the writing. Respect helps provide a basis for taking risks (and minimizing fear that obstructs access to our full intelligence), for clarifying and extending our thinking, and for engaging with the challenges involved in questioning, understanding, and communicating (see the snapshot on the 4Rs in Teaching and Learning for Reflective Practice, Part 4.) In this spirit, early in your process, you might:

• Read your **Paragraph Overview** to the group to hear how it sounds shared out loud with others (**Phase A**);

- Explain your project to your advisor and peers and respond to their questions or suggestions. This can work both to open wide and to focus in and formulate (**Phase C**). So that your train of thought can keep going without interruption, you might ask the other person to take notes and record highlights of what you say.
- Elicit comments on your **Narrative Outline** and **Drafts**, taking the opportunity to specify the way you would like to be responded to. Elbow and Belanoff (2000) provide a valuable summary of kinds of responses that ranges from "Read your piece aloud to listeners and ask: 'Would you please just listen and enjoy?'" through asking readers "What is almost said? What do you want to hear more about?" to providing readers with "specific criteria that you are wondering about or struggling with."

When you decide what approaches to commenting you ask for as a writer or what approaches you use as a commentator, keep Elbow and Belanoff's (2000) variety of responses in mind. (Elbow 1981, chapters 3 and 13 on sharing and feedback is relevant here as well.) After all, although some advisors (instructors) fill the margins with specific suggestions for clarification and changes, the response of students to the suggestions often goes no further than touching up —the desired re-thinking and revising of ideas and writing rarely happen. It seems a better use of an advisor's time to capture where the writer was taking you and make a few suggestions that might clarify and extend the impact on readers of what was written. As writers, we all value comments that show us that we have been listened to and our voice, however tentative, has been heard.

Small-Group Roles

The system below has two virtues missing from the common schemes that group leaders or teachers use to assign roles when they ask participants or students or participants to collaborate in small groups:
- the roles should not divert participants from participating in the activity; and
- everyone should have to reflect and synthesize what happened.

Roles:
Includer, Orienter, Phaser, Process Reporter.
There is no recorder or note-taker role. Everyone has the role of Participant in all phases.

Phases of small-group activity and specific roles active in that phase:

1) GETTING TOGETHER to begin activity	Includer, Orienter, Phaser
2) The main part of the ACTIVITY	Orienter, Includer, Phaser
3) SYNTHESIS and REFLECTION	Includer, Process Reporter, Phaser
4) REPORTING	Randomly chosen person, Process Reporter

Phase I - GETTING TOGETHER

to begin activity

Includer (to ensure participation)
- Choose a space and set up chairs so everyone can face each other and hear comfortably.
- Bring everyone into the group, not off to one side or facing the group on an angle.
- Make sure everyone in the group is introduced to others they might not know.
- Establish how you will take turns (e.g., raise hands to be recognized, take a card from a stack, etc.)

Orienter (to get and keep the Activity on track)
- Check that everyone knows their role.
- Check that everyone has read their own roles for the activity & understands which phases it applies to.
- Ask people to explain their roles to each other (so that everyone understands the other roles).
- Ask everyone to read (or reread) the activity.
- Give your version of the activity and goals, and then invite others to adjust or clarify your version.
- Check that everyone knows what's going on and why. If it's not clear after that, call for the instructor's attention.

INSERT DESCRIPTION OF ACTIVITY HERE

Phaser (to move group from one phase to the next in a timely manner)
- Remind people of how much time there is for the phases ahead.

Phase 2 – Main part of the ACTIVITY

Orienter
- Remind everyone that they should take notes to aid synthesis (of content) and reflection (on process).
- Initiate discussion of how to proceed so as to fulfill the goals of the activity.
- Watch for uncertainty or disagreement about how the group is proceeding.
- Call for the leader or instructor's attention when the group needs more guidance about where they are going.
- Gently interrupt if you think the group is diverging from the activity.

Includer
- Ensure everyone gets a chance to speak.
- Bring people back into the group when they have withdrawn (on their own or in a one-on-one discussion).

- Ask for time out for a check-in when withdrawal recurs or persists.
- Do something about distractions (e.g., a noisy cell phone user outside the classroom; hot room).

Phaser
- Watch time, prompting group to move onto next task of the activity and ensuring that clear time is left for the synthesis and reflection phase.

Everyone (individually)
- Make notes to aid synthesis (of content) and reflection (on process).
- Ask for time out if you feel that any of the roles need to be more actively pursued.

Phase 3 – SYNTHESIS and REFLECTION

(group members take stock of what they have learned during the activity, about both content and process)

Everyone (individually)
- Digest the content of the discussion, make notes on your own conclusions and open questions, and prepare for reporting or contributing to the report from the activity (if one is required).
- Digest the process of the activity.

Includer
- Check in quietly with anyone who has stalled in their synthesis and note-making.

Process Reporter (to synthesize stock-taking on the process)
- Ask everyone to mention one highlight or appreciation from the activity. Make notes.
- Ask everyone to mention one issue needing further work or

improvement from the *process* of the activity. Make notes.
• Prepare to report back on what you have noted. (This report is about the process. It is not a report about the activity if that is required.)

Phaser
• Remind people to be brief in their spoken feedback on the process.

Phase 4 – REPORTING

(either spoken to the whole group or given to instructor or leader, as requested)

Randomly chosen person (*not* the Process Reporter)
• Make presentation or draft a written report (if required).

Everyone (individually)
• Provide additions or modifications.

Process Reporter
• Report back on what you have noted about the process of the activity (e.g., highlights and suggested improvements).

Statistical Thinking

If you understand the simple chain of thinking below, you can enlist or hire a statistician who will use the appropriate recipe for the data you have.

1. There is a *population* of individuals (or entities). (Population = individuals subject to the same foreground causes of interest. There may also be background, non-manipulable causes that vary among these individuals.)

2. For some *measurable attribute* (e.g., height, income, test score) the individuals have responses to the foreground causes that *vary* (possibly because of the background causes).

3. You have *observations* of the measurable attribute for two or more subsets (samples) of the population.

4. *Central question* of statistical analysis: Are the subsets sufficiently different in their varying responses that you *doubt* that they are from the one population (that is, you doubt that they are subject to all the same foreground causes)? Statisticians answer this question with *recipes* that are variants of a comparison between the averages for the subsets in relation to the spread around the averages. The statisticians' comparison means that in the left hand situation below you are more likely to doubt that subsets A and B are from the same population.

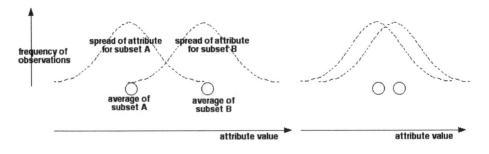

The central question of statistical analysis: Are the averages far apart relative to the spread (left hand picture) or not (right hand picture)?

146

5. If you doubt that the subsets are from the same population, you investigate further, drawing on other knowledge about the subsets. You hope to *expose the causes involved* and then take action informed by that knowledge about the causes.

Strategic Personal Planning

In order to complete a satisfying project you need to focus on something tight and do-able. Strategic Personal Planning allows you to arrive at this focus by first opening out and acknowledging a wide range of factors and wishes that your work could take into account.

Strategic Personal Planning is based on the strategic participatory planning workshop process developed by the Institute for Cultural Affairs (ICA; see Action Research and Participation in Part 4). The basic propositions of the ICA workshop process include the following:

• Notwithstanding any initial impressions to the contrary, everyone has insight (wisdom) and we need everyone's insight for the wisest result.

• There is insight in every response. There are no wrong answers.

• We know more than we are, at first, prepared or able to acknowledge.

• When we are heard, we can better hear others and hear ourselves. This causes us to examine decisions made in advance about what the other people are like, what they are and are not capable of.

• The step-by-step workshop process thus aims to keep us listening actively to each other, foster mutual respect, and elicit more of our insight.

• Our initial conclusions may change, so we need to be open for surprises.

• What we come out with is very likely to be larger and more durable than what any one person came in with; the more so, the more voices that are brought out by the process.

• In particular, we will be engaged in carrying out and carrying on the plans we develop.

• In sum, the workshop process aims for the "greatest input, with greatest commitment and the least confusion, in the least time."

To adapt these principles to Strategic *Personal* Planning means that you should hope to come out with a plan for your project that is richer, deeper, and has more dimensions than what you came in with. The more angles on yourself that are brought out by the process, the more likely you are to create something you did not anticipate. The experience of that creativity, in turn, leads you to be more likely to carry out the plan you arrive at.

The Strategic Personal Planning process begins with the "practical vision" stage. The idea is to generate a larger vision of your work that underlies the specific project you are undertaking. In that spirit, do not focus specifically on your project topic. Instead, consider a more global question: What is needed for your personal and professional development in [*insert here: general area required to be addressed by the project*]?

Steps

Post-it brainstorming

Imagine yourself some time after the project is over looking back with a sense of accomplishment on how far you have come in the area of [*insert general area required to be addressed by the project*]. (Construe *accomplishment* broadly so it can include your own reflection and growth.) What happened to make this so?—What different kinds of things do you envisage having gone into or contributed to that personal and professional development? In preparing for this brainstorming, take note of the following:
• These things can span the mundane and inspiring; tangible and intangible; process, as well as product; relationships as well as individual skills. (By *mundane*, think of all the different tasks on your plate —over and above those for this project—that potentially affect your ability to carry out your project in a way that is satisfying.)
• Reread any externally-dictated context and requirements for the project (e.g., the description, objectives, or expectations given in a course syllabus).

Keeping in mind the question above, brainstorm your three to five word answers onto Post-its in block letters. (Alternatively, on your computer, you can make virtual Post-its that you can move around.)

Pair up and get more ideas from hearing about the kinds of things the other person came up with. Make more Post-its. Once you have about 30 Post-its, move to the next phase.

Clustering and Naming

• Move the Post-its around into groups of items that have something in common *in the way they address the question*.
• Describe the groups *using a phrase that has a verb in it* or, at least, indicates some action. For example, instead of "Holistic Artistic Survival Project," an active name would be "Moving Holistically from Surviving to Thriving as Artists."
• Group the groups in pairs or threes and give these larger groups descriptive active names.
• Group these groups and name them, until you arrive at a descriptive active name for the practical vision Post-its as a whole.

(The diagrams below illustrate the naming of the original groups of Post-its and the subsequent grouping and naming of larger groups. These clusters and names were developed using Post-its [not shown] brainstormed by an entire class on the question of what was needed for their continuing personal and professional development at the end of a course on **Action Research** and Educational Evaluation.)

Pair up again and discuss your overall vision.

After the session, redraw the groups in a neat form (without the original Post-its) so you can refer back to the vision chart as you define and undertake your project.

Translate Strategic Personal Planning into a concrete Research and Engagement Design

Quick option: **Freewrite** (for 7-10 minutes) on the specific actions you might take so as to complete a project that fulfills your practical vision as well as meets any more specific objectives and expectations. Keep these action ideas in sight, together with your practical vision, as you plan the remainder of your work.

More time-consuming option: Pursue the other three stages of Strategic Personal Planning, starting with brainstorming on the obstacles to your realizing this vision. Re-vision those obstacles (perhaps with peer or advisor interaction) until you see the underlying issues and a gateway through to new, strategic directions, and then to specific actions that follow those directions.

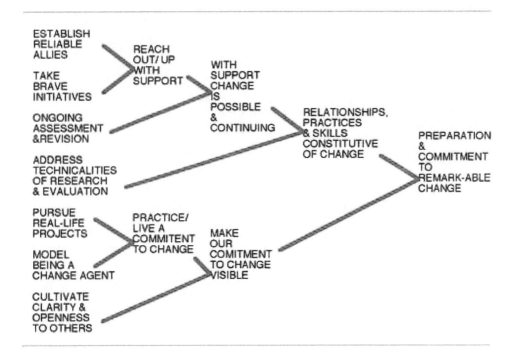

```
Look to develop
Purpose to Life                          I
------------------    ---------    I  Changing
Attitude of Openness              I  with Others
to Change           I  Value Others I  can give    I
------------------  I  because this I  Life         I  Be Open &
Interest in         I  can Change   I  a Purpose    I  Make Effort
Contributions of    I  You                          I  Needed for
Others                                              I  Personal      I
------------------     ---------       --------     I  Change        I
Persist in Self-                                    I               I  Openness
Reflection Activities I  Bring Out                  I               I  —within
------------------    I  one's Voice  I  Through    I               I  and to
Develop Skills in     I  and Others'  I  Discipline I               I  others'
Working with Others                   I  Voice &                    I  creativity
------------------       ---------    I  Competency                 I  —
Maintain Focus                        I  Emerge                     I  &
(within complexity)   I  Competency  I                              I  Disciplin'd
------------------    I  in/and Focus                               I  Focus
Practice Using Tools  I                                             I  need to be
------------------       ----------      ---------      -------     I  Combined
Seek out good         Build                                         I  to become
Facilitation of Group I  Supportive                                 I  an Agent
Work                  I  Connections,                               I  of Change-
------------------    I  incl.                       I  Look for    I  in-
Build Supportive      I  Facilitation                I  Support &   I  Collabor-
Connections              for Group                   I  Opportun-   I  ation
                         Work                         I  ities to    I
------------------       ----------      --------     I  Collaborate
Experience            Positive                       I  &
Participation         I  Experience   Take up        I  Participate
Positively            I  for oneself- I  Opportun-   I
------------------    I  in-          I  ities that  I
Tap into one's        I  collaboratn. I  might give
Creative Energies                     I  Experiences
------------------       --------     I  in Real-Life
Engaged in real                       I  Situations
(workplace) Situations
```

Naming of the original groups of Post-its and subsequent grouping and naming of larger groups. (Based on Post-it brainstorming by two classes concerning what is needed for their continuing personal and professional development at the end of a course on Action Research and Educational Evaluation)

Support and Coaching Structure

By what means can the group function as a support and coaching structure to get most participants (e.g., students) to finish their research and writing in the time available? That is a question worth discussing during any process of research, writing, and engagement. (See the Resources section in Part 4 for an online forum on this topic.)

Background premises: Individually and in a group of peer students or researchers, you already know a lot about research and engagement. If this knowledge is elicited and affirmed, you are more able to learn from others. Activities such as **Freewriting** bring to the surface insight that you were not able, at first, to acknowledge. Over the course of the research and writing process, you are encouraged to recognize that there is insight in every response and share their not-yet-stable aspects. The trust required takes time to establish.

An email group (listserv) can be used to help the community develop, but these often end up used more for logistics (e.g., noting that such and such a webpage or wiki link is broken). To generate more interaction, a survey given a few sessions in from the start can provide material for a practical vision process (along the lines of **Strategic Personal Planning**, but with a small group instead of a single individual doing the brainstorming, clustering, and naming) (Taylor 1999).

Supportive Listening

Supportive Listening, which is similar to the constructivist listening of Weissglass (1990), is a practice you may wish to include as a routine at the start of group meetings or course sessions so everyone gets fully present.

• Split into pairs. Each person has half the time available to be listened to and, even if not talking, to simply be paid attention to.
• The listener may offer supportive words, but should not interrupt or bring in their own experience. It is enough just to be listening attentively and non-judgementally.
• Being listened to in this way helps you move through what is distracting you from being clear. It is a way of moving you towards a place where you are able to take initiative in new ways.
• Just having someone listen to you with no strings attached can bring up strong feelings. Although this can be scary, see it as a positive experience. Try not to damp down these feelings or be embarrassed by them.
• Supportive listening is done in absolute confidentiality. Afterwards, the listeners must not refer to what is said to anyone, not even to the person who said it.

The context determines the topic, e.g., "looking ahead to making a public presentation of my research next week." However, as is the case of **Freewriting**, it is OK—indeed important—to let the topic be eclipsed by preoccupations from work and life.

Ten Questions

State your topic. Write down ten questions within that topic. Circle two that interest you the most. Take these two and list ten questions under each. Circle two that interest you the most. Based on those two questions, define or refine the **Governing Question** that conveys what you need to research (and clarifies what you no longer need to research).

(see **Phase C**)

Think-Pair-Share

Think-Pair-Share is a simple practice that ensures everyone has a chance to formulate and air their thinking, not only the people who readily speak up in groups.

- *Think*—prepare your thoughts on your own (in response to guidelines given by the group leader or instructor), then
- *Pair* up with another person, and, through sharing ideas verbally, refine them and prepare to
- *Share* a key part of your ideas with the whole group, which you do when called on by the group facilitator (or instructor).

Visual Aids

Visual Aids should *aid* your presentation, not duplicate it or distract from it. Indeed, use of simple, readily assimilated visuals can allow you to provide a quick overview and essential background for the project, freeing you up to use most of your time to focus on the areas in which you need most feedback.

Tips

The following apply just as much to PowerPoint slides as to old-fashioned overhead transparencies:
• Include only key words or prompts to what you are going to say
• 15-25 words only on any one visual
• 1/2 inch (1.25cm) high text or larger
• Design your Visual Aids not on full size sheets, but inside quadrants of a single sheet of paper divided into four parts. Print your words in these quadrants, then scale up to the actual visual aid. This approach ensures that you will not squeeze too much text in one slide.
• Be wary of bullet points (except when the topic is a list of items such as these tips).
• (The typical problem with bullets is that, even when all of the points may be relevant and interesting, the variety of the way the points are phrased and their order does not convey a flow in which each point prepares the way for the one that follows. If you are accustomed to making points in bullet form, ask a peer or your advisor to take notes as you practice speaking the words that explain your bullets. Then use those notes to rephrase and order the bullets so the flow or logic is evident in the visual, that is, can be taken in without your spoken narrative.
• Practice your presentation using the Visual Aids in front of a peer who is given specific instructions to note when the Visuals Aids interfere—not aid—or are not referred to.

> Key words & prompts only
>
> To design: PRINT on ¼ sheet
>
> 15-25 words only
>
> Text > ½" (1.25cm)
>
> Avoid bullet points
>
> Peer checks: Visuals *aid*?

A visual aid on tips for the preparation of visual aids (not to scale)

Work-in-Progress Presentation

When you prepare (e.g., by **Freewriting** or designing **Visual Aids**) to give a presentation, when you hear yourselves deliver your presentations, and when you get feedback, it usually leads to self-clarification of the **Overall Argument** underlying your research and the eventual written reports. This, in turn, influences your priorities (see **Research Design**) for the time remaining. Presentations a little over half way through the project must necessarily be on work-in-progress, so you have to indicate where additional research is needed and where you think it might lead you.

The Work-in-Progress Presentation is your first opportunity to "**GOSP**" your audience. Note that, for a Work-in-Progress Presentation, the P in GOSP—*position*—may extend to include your *plans* to find out what more you need to. At the same time, think of the presentation less in terms of performing to the public and more in terms of getting the help you need from others to make further progress. In that spirit, make sure you allow time to present the *leading edge* of your work. That means you need to be economical in how you get listeners up to steam about the aspects of your project that you already have firmly in place.

If there is no time for extensive discussion, each member of the audience should write a **Plus-Delta** note to the presenter to provide appreciations, questions, or suggestions, which might include contacts and references.

(see **Phase G**)

Writing Groups for Support and Feedback

A small group—three people is a good number—finds a regular time each week that *every member* can protect from *all* other distractions. You commit to taking turns from one meeting to the next to receive feedback on the latest installment of your writing, which should be precirculated at least 2 days before the meeting along with a note about the kind of feedback desired (see Elbow and Belanoff 2000). The groups are, of course, free to establish additional forms of support beyond giving feedback on writing.

Writing Preferences

Not everyone follows the same process for arranging thoughts and putting them down in words. It is valuable to identify the kind of writing process you generally use. When you understand the strengths of your approach, you may keep them in mind as resources to capitalise on. When you see the limitations, you may take compensatory measures (e.g., build in time after your complete a first draft for **Reverse Outlining** and thoroughgoing revision) or undertake remedial exercises to bring alternative approaches into your toolkit.

One way to explore writing preferences is to position yourself in relation to one of each of four pairs of profiles that Legendre (n.d.), a writing instructor at Cornell University, created based on Myers-Briggs personality types.

(see **Phase G**)

Writing Workshop

If you are working to the same completion date as a number of peers, a regular hour-long Writing Workshop that moves through the five phases below allows you to report on your progress and to reflect on topics that can be crafted by the facilitator (instructor) to correspond to the likely issues for each stage in the research and writing process.

1. **Freewriting** with two goals: To get present (clearing away distracting concerns from your busy lives); and to begin to consider the topic of the session.

2. **Check-In**: One thing that is on top for you as you come into the workshop. It may be a concern or question about the topic of the session, or it may be something else going on for you.

3. **Dialogue Process**: Structured turn-taking that builds on what is said in the check-in about the topic of the session. Through inquiry more than advocacy—including inquiry of one's own thinking—themes usually emerge. The facilitator participates but, if needed, reminds participants to build on what speakers have said (as against rehearsing positions established before the session). Continue turn-taking until seven minutes before the session ends.

4. Writing to gather thoughts: Spend a few minutes writing down what has emerged that is most meaningful for you.

5. **Closing Circle**: Share something you plan to address or get done or think more about based on the Workshop session. Airing this in the group-having it witnessed-makes it more likely to happen.

Meetings of peer **Writing Groups for Support and Feedback** and **One-on-one Sessions** with the advisor might follow the Workshop hour.

Written Evaluation, at End of a Project or Course

This is written as a course evaluation, but the same format can be used for a workshop or an extended process of research supervised by an advisor. The wording needs to be adapted in various places to match the specific course or project.

Part I

The primary goal here is to make notes as preparation for Part II, a synthetic statement. Nevertheless, try to be legible because some reviewers might read Part I as well.

1. Start with a self-evaluation:

Did you achieve your personal goals? How would you have proceeded differently if you were doing this course again? What have been your major personal obstacles to learning more from this course?

What have you learned about making a workshop format course stimulating and productive? What would your advice be to prospective students about how to get the most from a course like this?

2. General evaluation:

How did the course meet or not meet your expectations? How did your attitude to doing the course change through the semester? How do you think the course could be improved? What was special about this course (+positive & -negative)? How does it compare with other courses? What would be your overall recommendation to prospective students?

3. Evaluation in relation to the course description:

Comment on how well the goals expressed there were met and make general and specific suggestions about how these could be better met. From the syllabus:

> (e.g., http://www.faculty.umb.edu/pjt/692-08.html: In this course you identify a current social or educational issue that concerns you—you want to know more about it, advocate a change, design a curriculum unit or a workshop, and so on. You work through the different phases of research and engaging others on that issue—from envisioning a manageable project to communicating your findings and plans for further work. If you are a CCT student, you should integrate perspectives from your previous CCT courses and will end up well prepared for—or well underway in—your synthesis project.
>
> The classes run as workshops, in which you are introduced to and then practice using tools for research, communicating, and developing as a reflective practitioner. The class activities and course as a whole provide models for guiding your own students or supervisees in systematically addressing issues that concern them.

Part II

Write out neatly a synthetic statement (1 or 2 paragraphs) evaluating this course. (You might build on or build in your comments from part I.) Please make comments both to help the instructor develop the course in the future and to enable some third party appreciate the course's strengths and weaknesses. (Imagine a reader who may not be willing to wade through all the notes on the other side, but is willing to do more than look at numerical averages.) Among other things you might comment on...*fill in key features of the course (e.g., the overall content and progression of classes, the Phases of Research and Engagement, and the in-class activities).*

3
ILLUSTRATIONS

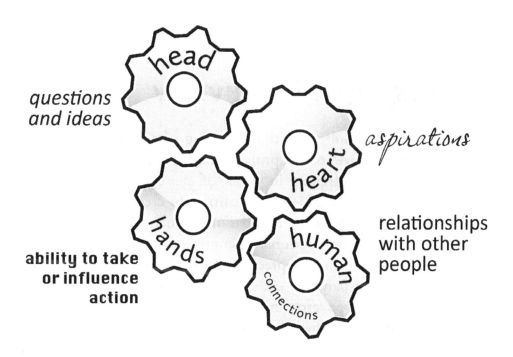

questions
and ideas

aspirations

relationships
with other
people

ability to take
or influence
action

ILLUSTRATION of PHASES

Work In Progress for a Project on Engaging Adult Learning Communities in Using The Principles of Theater Arts to Prepare Them to Create Social Change, Phase A

Governing Question

What are the steps that I can take to engage the adult learning communities in using the principles of theater arts to prepare them to create social change?

Paragraph Overview

Within modern adult education, learning often addresses the skills needed to improve one's professional opportunities or increase knowledge and awareness in areas of personal interest. Another outcome can be to enable adult learners to create social change by developing key skills at the foundation of such change. These skills may include interpersonal communication, collaboration, community organizing, appreciation for diversity and alternative cultures, and expanded use of imagination. Complex social challenges such as poverty, injustice, and poor health may be more effectively addressed when the individuals with these skills use them to find a collective understanding of the underlying issues. Further, the process of change must have ownership by all within the community and particularly be inclusive of those without power, influence or status. I am particularly interested in the ways that adult learning communities may employ the principles of the theater arts as a strategy for introducing and reinforcing the key skills, without requiring that the participants have formal exposure to theater or social activism. I would like to develop methodologies that both use theater as a foundation for learning and are most appropriate for adult education forums. Further, I hope to understand how to introduce and advocate those methodologies to organizations, community groups, and individuals that seek social change, drawing upon my own experiences in adult education at social service agencies. By using principles such as storytelling, character development, role-playing, point-of-view, methodological belief, monologue and dialogue, directing, and empathy, I hope to help construct a perspective of adult education that represents an alternative to the traditional classroom, supports participation from diverse groups, and creates a truly enjoyable learning experience that better prepares adults to meet the most critical issues of their social environment.

Work In Progress for a Project on Engaging Adult Learning Communities in Using The Principles of Theater Arts to Prepare Them to Create Social Change, Phase B

Annotated Bibliography

Governing Question: What are the steps that I can take to engage the adult learning communities in using the principles of theater arts to prepare them to create social change?

(excerpts only)

Subheading 1: *The following works that reflect the end goal of social change through a more revolutionary viewpoint of what "adult education" should really mean, and the involvement of community members in participatory theater:*

<u>Key Readings</u>

1. Freire, Paulo (1968). Pedagogy of the Oppressed. New York: Seabury Press.

• Freire is considered one of the fathers of the formulation of adult education theory with respect to helping those oppressed and developed the idea of "popular education", the technique of using learning to help individuals understand how their own actions and situations connect to those of the community. Many other works in this bibliography draw upon Freire's work.

2. Boal: Augusto (1979). Theater of the Oppressed. New York: Urizen.

• Boal is a follower of Freire and built upon his work more specifically in terms of using drama and participatory theater in the search for allowing individuals to develop social change. This work is fundamental to almost all other cited works below that address the use of theater in adult education communities to enable social change.

3. KEY ARTICLE: Desai, Guarev. (1990). Theater as Praxis: Discursive Strategies in African Popular Theater. African Studies Review, Vol. 33, No. 1, April 1990, pp. 65-92.

This article provides a historical context for the idea of the Theater of the Oppressed and discusses the use of participatory theater in African countries to develop the adult education system into what is seen as its most critical format, which is to help the people become educated about basic-needs issues such as health and interacting with the government power structure. Although certainly not a complete survey of all issues related to my topic, I chose this as a key article because it represents one way in which the theater arts, social change, and adult education are considered a single unified idea and not simply a hybrid of others; also, historical examples discussed demonstrate how all members of a community are involved as valued participants, particularly those who do not have formal experience in theater, teaching, or activism. This is an underlying requirement to the assumptions guiding my Governing Question.

<u>Supplemental Readings and Case Studies</u>
The following readings are supplements to the works listed above and build upon the work of Freire and Boal:
• Cohen-Cruz, J. (1993). Playing Boal: Theatre of the Oppressed Anthology. New York: Routledge.
• Schipani, Daniel (1984). Conscientization and Creativity. Lanham, MD: University Press of America, Inc.
• Carter Ogden, Jean (1983). Everyman's drama;: A study of the noncommercial theatre in the United States. New York: American Association for Adult Education.
• Cohen-Cruz, J. (2005). Local Acts: Community-based Performance In The United States. New Brunswick, NJ: Rutgers University Press.

The following articles all serve a similar purpose and provide case studies of the use of Theater Develop for serving the adult learning communities in specific social issues:
• Frey, L. and Carragee, K. (2006). Catalyzing Social Reform Through Participatory Folk Performances in Rural India. Communication and Social Activism, Cresskill, NJ: Hampton Press.

• Kemp, Martin (2006). Promoting the Health and Wellbeing of Young Black Men Using Community-Based Drama. Health Education, Volume 106, Issue 3. pp. 186-200.
• Ndumbe Eyoh, Hansel (1987). Theatre and Community Education: The Africa Experience. Africa Media Review, Vol. 1, No. 3, pp 56-68.
• Conrad, Diane (2004). Exploring Risky Youth Experiences: Popular Theatre as a Participatory Performative Research Method. International Journal of Qualitative Methods, Vol. 3, Issue 1, April 2004.
• Malamah-Thomas, D. (1987). Theatre Development in Sierra Leone: A Study of Care's Project Learn. Africa Media Review Vol. 1, No. 3.

Similar bibliographic lists appear for the following additional subheadings:
Subheading 2: The following works connect ideas of teaching directly to use of theater techniques
and
Subheading 3: The following works address the meaning of teaching and theater toward social change

Work In Progress for a Project on Engaging Adult Learning Communities in Using The Principles of Theater Arts to Prepare Them to Create Social Change, Phase C

Revised Map

Governing Question: What are the steps that I can take to engage the adult learning communities in using the principles of theater arts to prepare them to create social change?

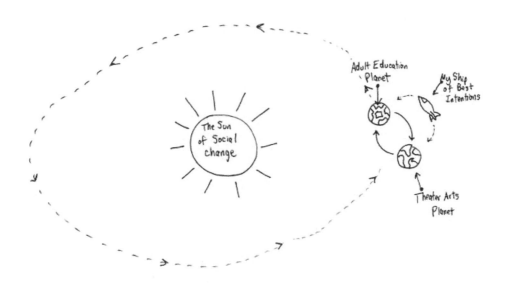

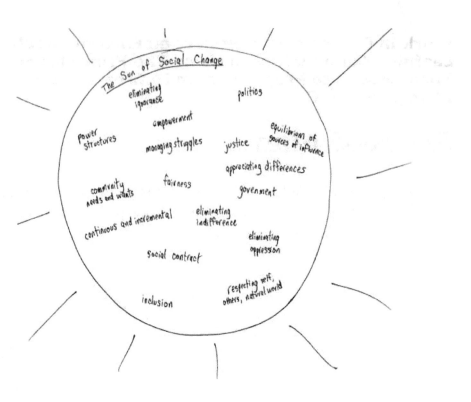

The Sun of Social Change

eliminating
ignorance

politics

empowerment

power
structures

equilibrium of
sources of influence

managing struggles   justice

appreciating differences

community
needs and wants

fairness

govenment

continuous and incremental

eliminating
indifference

eliminating
oppression

social contract

respecting self,
others, natural world

inclusion

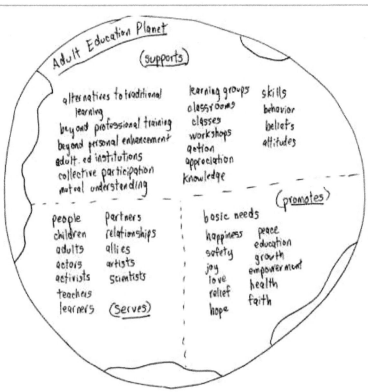

Adult Education Planet

(supports)

alternatives to traditional
learning
beyond professional training
beyond personal enhancement
adult. ed institutions
collective participation
mutual understanding

learning groups   skills
classrooms   behavior
classes   beliefs
workshops   attitudes
action
appreciation
knowledge

(promotes)

people   partners   basic needs
children   relationships happiness   peace
adults   allies   safety   education
actors   artists   joy   growth
activists scientists   love   empowerment
teachers   relief   health
learners   (serves)   hope   faith

172

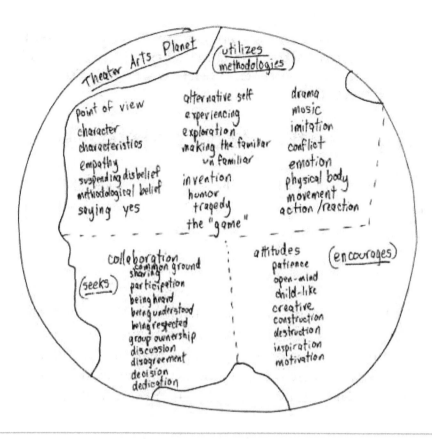

Theater Arts Planet (utilizes methodologies)

Point of view
character
characteristics
empathy
suspending disbelief
methodological belief
saying yes

alternative self
experiencing
exploration
making the familiar
un familiar
invention
humor
tragedy
the "game"

drama
music
imitation
conflict
emotion
physical body
movement
action/reaction

(seeks) collaboration
common ground
sharing
participation
being heard
being understood
being respected
group ownership
discussion
disagreement
decision
dedication

attitudes (encourages)
patience
open-mind
child-like
creative
construction
destruction
inspiration
motivation

My Role: Creating Relationships Between Adult Education Planet and Theater Arts Planet and Facilitate How Each Can Share Resources with the Other through:

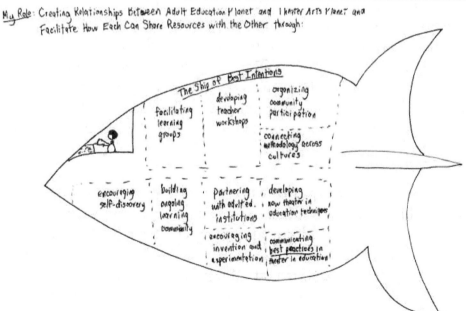

The Ship of Best Intentions

facilitating
learning
groups

developing
teacher
workshops

organizing
community
participation

connecting
methodology across
cultures

encouraging
self-discovery

building
ongoing
learning
community

partnering
with adult ed.
institutions

developing
new theater in
education techniques

encouraging
invention and
experimentation

communicating
best practices in
theater in education

Work In Progress for a Project on Engaging Adult Learning Communities in Using The Principles of Theater Arts to Prepare Them to Create Social Change, Phase D

Component Propositions

Governing Question: What are the steps that I can take to engage the adult learning communities in using the principles of theater arts to prepare them to create social change?

Proposition 1: Theater provides methodologies that can support how adult learners become better prepared to become engaged in social change. Concepts such as characterization, point-of-view, methodological belief, use of physical movement and props, and dialogue can be adapted to situations that are encountered in everyday life and therefore are not simply tools that drive the theater performance industry but also reflect social realism.

Counter-proposition: Overwhelmingly, theater is perceived primarily as a source of entertainment or as a "soft skill" and will not be taken seriously as a medium of authentic foundation of education. Because much education addresses the learning that is meant to support decision-making and problem-solving, these are often part of situations that require well-defined "right" answers, and theater methodologies don't insist upon this, so they may not be useful.

Counter-counter-proposition: Theater is perceived as primarily entertaining because it often represents a "reward" to the passive observer that is earned for doing other "real" work, but using theater methodologies in education takes a different form anyway because teachers, learners, and educational administrators can use the methodologies in numerous ways that form a foundation of interpersonal interaction, communication, originality, and creativity. There needs to be more emphasis on these as achievable milestones in education alongside those reflecting technical skills.

Proposition 2: Social change happens when all people have an opportunity to have ownership and participation in the processes that enable it, and people must be able to form a common understanding about the issues that they mean to address.

Counter-proposition: Because those most affected by broad social challenges lack power and influence in the first place, social change must be enacted through political means and relies on government action to create any lasting change. A social challenge such as poverty is extremely far-reaching and deeply problematic, so any educational approach to addressing the issue will require decisions by a representative group, since it is logistically difficult to have direct involvement from large numbers of people.

Counter-counter-proposition: Reliance on government and political action to create social change causes a disconnect between the decision makers and the members of the community; it permits a certain degree on dependence on those who are only indirectly involved in the specific issues that they are trying to address. True change must start at the individual level through education and motivation to become personally involved in the changes that will affect the individuals' own lives. This individual change must then be used to build local-level perspectives on social change.

Proposition 3: A key purpose of adult education is that people, through learning experiences, will be more able to address the most immediate and critical issues affecting the basic needs that are common to all people, not just themselves, such as justice, safety, and good health.

Counter-proposition: In our current economic climate, a people need to have the professional skills to be competitive in a global economy. Adult education needs to become an innovator of training toward best practices in business, engineering, and medical and scientific research. Although awareness of social issues is important, the emphasis of adult education must be in the preparation of people to have these critical skills.

Counter-counter-proposition: Social change needs to be viewed as a more fundamental goal of a community of people because the most pressing social issues compound over time and become more complicated and devastating if not addressed. Therefore, adult education must teach toward social change as an underlying purpose, and this needs to be the reason for scientists, businesspeople, engineers, etc., to actually be doing the work they do. Because education toward social change is more fundamentally critical to a strong society, this must be encouraged at a level equal to or even greater than education toward economic power. Further, because education toward social change is relevant to all people no matter what other occupation they take, this needs to be a common thread of one's education all the way through adulthood.

Proposition 4: The theater techniques that are appropriate for teaching social change-oriented skills are accessible to all people, easy to learn, and draw upon abilities that are natural and enjoyable for people to express, regardless of their level of specific academic experience. People are capable of understanding and using these techniques in their own education and also capable of becoming developers of new techniques that can be effecting in teaching that prepares one with the skills needed for social change.

Counter-proposition: Although both theater and adult education may seem extremely familiar to most people, particularly in North American culture, it takes specialized training in theater to understand concepts such as directing, developing characters, using dialogue effectively, and establishing in oneself a new point of view. Likewise, it take specialized training in education to understand concepts of andragogy/pedagogy, transformational education, organizational management, and curriculum development, design, delivery, and evaluation. Those with such training are much more capable of leading learning experiences that have valid effects.

Counter-counter proposition: Using the techniques of theater in adult education is not meant to produce professional actors or activists, but rather to find the techniques that generally help a person to learn how to take on different perspectives of themselves and others, use empathy to understand difficulties of others that lie outside of their own lives, and explore different notions of reality that may help to stimulate imagination and create vision for an approach to addressing social issues that doesn't yet exist and may be obscured but that might be possible. From this point of view, the use of theater is not intended to create a skill that leads to performance for others but instead leads to a more inward change to reflect upon the reality of one's own perception of the world, understanding of the social structure in which one lives, and the actions that one can take to create change of that structure that most directly influences the individual and the immediate community.

Work In Progress for a Project on Engaging Adult Learning Communities in Using The Principles of Theater Arts to Prepare Them to Create Social Change, Phase E

Strategic Personal Planning

Governing Question: What are the steps that I can take to engage the adult learning communities in using the principles of theater arts to prepare them to create social change?

The theme of all of my strategic personal planning is to more effectively narrow my attention to the realistic achievements within my research for the next few months. Generally, I have felt that my research has often expanded rather than contracted, so I have at times become lost in the breadth and depth of research material and have found it rewarding to explore that even though I have also needed time to manage my research process. At this point, a main theme of my continued research is to be satisfied with my accomplishment so far and also be dedicated to the concrete tasks that need to be finished for my final paper/project.

Current status:
1. class assignments A-E completed, meaning that I now have a clear research bibliography that I am using to focus my exploration

2. developed a clear notetaking system for my research materials; I have defined a set of subtopics of my research that help me to organize my broad ideas, so now it has become easier to focus my attention on the research, since many of the resources are lengthy books rather than articles. I have spent much time reading but have experienced slow progress because the volume of possible reading is very high. My system of organization is allowing me to selectively choose reading in a more efficient way.

3. I have done some significant work regarding interviewing/visiting relevant to my project. This has included three phone interviews so far and a visit to a theater-based education program. There are two more visits/conversations pending regarding other use of applied theater in social change education. I have come to realize more that this process of finding "allies" and organizations in my search for applications of theater in education toward social change is simply an ongoing process of all of my future work, so I will need to start to consider this more outside of the construct of the Research and Engagement course. In a way, I feel like the expansion of my own involvement in the greater community is itself an ultimate outcome that I have needed from the course. I still need to complete my write-up of the interactions mentioned above.

<u>Areas of greatest priority for upcoming months</u>:
1. Shift from spending time reading, interviewing, and reflecting to writing instead. Because I have so many different ideas and thoughts about ways of thinking about my research, it is vitally important to continue to fill out the outline of my research paper with more and more detail and finish my first draft within the next few weeks.

2. Find ways to engage with the other members of the class to work out the remaining questions and challenges to my assumptions. After our upcoming discussion of peer support, I hope to establish at least one "partner" in class with which to share work and offer encouragement.

3. Share my current progress with others in a more regular way. One of my goals for myself was to find ways to include others more in my work, and I've found that I need to return to a more basic level of interaction that can move away from the "weight" of research that I've done. One way to do this is to talk about the enjoyment of learning with the adults in my workplace and hear more personal stories about what makes learning fun for them. Also, I will plan to speak more with those in my improv. class about rewarding parts of the class.

<u>Obstacles to moving forward</u>:

1. Obstacle: As I have continued researching, I have found additional resources that seem relevant, but it is too easy to become involved in their depths, and this takes time. The underlying obstacle is that I feel the need to explore every resource even though there really is not enough time to do so. This seems related to my enthusiasm to learn more and more, which involves some difficult feelings because I realize that I can't spend all of my time in that way.

• Way to address this: I have now formed a revised bibliography, so now I feel that I must remain within that and trust that my resources are highly sufficient even if not globally representative of all of the ideas that I would like to explore. Also equally importantly, I have found that my interactions with others who engage in theater, education, and social change have been extremely fulfilling and have given me a practical view of this area that encourages me to move beyond the written research.

2. Obstacle: I find myself with limited time in terms of my classwork, day job, work as a graduate assistant, and other professional interests. In each of these cases, there is designated time to be physically present in each situation, but the nature of each also encourages some thought before and after. In my "in-between" times, there is competition between my attention to each of these areas, and it can be a struggle to focus on one at a time.

• Way to address this: I have decided to define a literal schedule of my free time in terms of which of these areas can be reasonably addressed within that time. For example, I have set my time of Saturday morning between 10:00am-12:00noon for reading and note-taking for one of my classes, and I have designated the times for other activities as well. This has allowed me to discipline myself to confine my thoughts to certain areas and be less distracted.

3. Obstacle: I had some multiple/redundant note-taking systems that were taking too much time to manage.

• Way to address this: I have now consolidated my note-taking system and now organize all of my work electronically. Originally, I felt that by writing everything by hand first and then transferring it to the computer, I was giving myself an opportunity for revision and reflection during that task and therefore would find new meaning in my notes/writing/planning. Now, I have established single computer files for each kind of related idea and enter new writings here directly (when possible). Even though I still benefit from hand-written notes as needed, I have had computer experience far long enough to most naturally find organization with computer files and still allow myself the flexibility of revision. For example, typing my weekly class journal in a single file actually makes it much each to review entries from previous weeks and make sense of my current reflections, so the whole process is much more clear and does not feel disjointed, which is what I experienced when taking notes first by hand all of the time.

Clear steps and tasks to continue my work (to be completed no later than the week of session 12):
1. complete my remaining phone discussions with those involved in adult ed. using theater principles.
2. review web sites of my list of relevant local organizations that integrate theater, education, and attention to social issues.
3. seek a workshop or class for future attendance regarding directing theater
4. review my notes/documentation from my previous CCT classes and include core ideas in my electronic notes
5. write out at least 3 examples of my own ideas for activities that involve using theater in a classroom setting to teach a social change concept, as a foundation for further experimentation, dialogue, and discussion (for possible inclusion in final paper)
6. develop a basic outline for a teacher education workshop which introduces the idea of theater activities into the adult education environment and specifies timing, goals, and suggested flow of the workshop.

Work In Progress for a Project on Engaging Adult Learning Communities in Using The Principles of Theater Arts to Prepare Them to Create Social Change, Phase F

Interview Guide

Governing Question: What are the steps that I can take to engage the adult learning communities in using the principles of theater arts to prepare them to create social change?

Introduction:

a. thank the interviewee for their time and confirm the allotted time to which we had agreed for this interview

b. provide a brief description of my purposes and research:

1) exploring the question of how use of theater arts can be used in adult education environments to support learning that prepares adults to create social change

2) brief explanation of Critical and Creative Thinking program

3) ask interviewee to explain their role in their organization/work situation

Questions:

Theater in Education

1. When you were first starting to involve yourself in the use of theater in education, what had you done to prepare yourself (informal and formal education)? In what ways do you wish you had been more prepared?

2. Can you tell me about successful work experience that gave you a new excitement or encouragement about the potential of this work?

3. What are the objections that have been expressed by your potential clients/constituents when you have suggested how your work and methods might be useful in their environment?

4. What have you done to form collaboration with others toward using applied theater in education? How have the skills of others

complemented your own?

Theater in Social Change Issues
5. Do you think that there are any key misconceptions that are broadly held about theater for social change?
6. *If you believe that that use of theater techniques in social change should be more prevalent in educational environments, what have been the barriers to making that happen?

Work Organization and Administration of the Program/Project
7. How do you organize the information that you need to manage your work?
8. What are the things that you need the most right now that would make your work most successful or fulfilling?
9. What are the most difficult parts of this work, especially the things that others may not tell me?
10. What do you do to keep up with the trends in the use of theater for social change and its educational applications?
11. *Are there any philosophical differences between you and your partners/staff in the way that you approach your goals? If so, how do you handle those?
12. * In terms of your daily work tasks, what are the parts that tend to be particularly boring or frustrating?

Additional Leads and Suggestions
13. Who are the other key people in the Boston area that might be able to provide insight or support?
14. Is there anything else that I should know?

Wrap-up

a. thank the interviewee for their time
b. mention how I will follow up with them, if appropriate
c. confirm again my support of the interviewee's work and efforts

Other Reminders:
1. monitor the time throughout the interview

2. when possible, think about how to phrase my next question in a way that also acknowledges the previous statement or comment - change the question order as needed

*I consider some of the questions to be "secondary" if pressed for time and needing to sacrifice some; these may also be answered or addressed in the course of discussing the other questions.

Work In Progress for a Project on Engaging Adult Learning Communities in Using The Principles of Theater Arts to Prepare Them to Create Social Change, Phase G

Work-in-progress Presentation

Governing Question: What are the steps that I can take to engage the adult learning communities in using the principles of theater arts to prepare them to create social change?

(text only; no visuals)
Presentation Title: "Bringing the fun back to adult learning through theater-based education towards emerging priorities"

Initial Assumptions and Perspectives
1. three different major elements of this question: theater arts, adult education, and social change

2. meanings: social change refers to the ways that a community comes to agreement upon social challenges and the way that they approach the decision-making and action needed to address them; could include the areas of health and safety, preventing crime and violence, awareness of broader issues of the environment, employment fairness, and access to education; adult education includes the learning environments in which adults intentionally find opportunities to define goals and take part in learning to reach them; theater arts include the types of performance that involve any use of voice, body, staging, and props to create an alternative reality

3. main idea is that there is a way in which adults can take on a view that ongoing education is enjoyable, and that it can serve a purpose beyond professional skills training or personal life enhancement; education can be structured to help people to structure their learning so that as well as it benefiting themselves, it

also can enable their individual abilities to complement each other toward an improvement of their entire community and world; to me, many principles of the theater arts support this because they can help people to understand alternative points of view, find greater empathy for the ideas of others that they don't originally understand or appreciate, find common ground with others, and become more aware of how their own attitudes influence the way that their actions affect others; also, theater arts provide a very natural way to practice the actions that might be part of social change in a safe environment, as a lead-in to actually taking action in their real lives

Research findings and Activities
1. The connection between theater and social change has been well-established, particularly in Africa and Latin America. The use of ideas such as "Theater of the Oppressed" and its derivatives like forum theater and popular education have used theater in public settings to create awareness and knowledge of many issues - disease prevention, dealing with military/police brutality, water cleanliness, and parenting skills. A fundamental need of this theater is that it is participatory - there is no separate actors/audience - all people can take roles "on stage." Also, formal acting training is not needed for participation.

2. Through some of my reading, interviews, and discussions, current practice of using theater in social change in the U.S. is often more narrow - these efforts tend to be designed and initiated by experts in theater but are often presented to organizational clients in the form of leadership training or workplace collaboration. The people that do this are practitioners who are providing a service to organizational clients, or sometimes as performance-based activities for schools.

3. There is much more to be realized in the way that theater arts may be introduced as a tool in teacher education. The greatest need seems to be to provide ways for the adult learning community to be aware of how the theater arts can benefit them and

understand how such methodologies can be connected directly to how the learning experience is helping to establish the skills that enable social change.

New Ideas
1. subversive view of "adult education" - traditionally focused on professional skills training and continuing education in the traditional of personal life enhancement - see a view in which adult. ed. becomes most strongly associated with social change

2. believe that the "methodologies of theater arts" are actually more fundamental aspects of human behavior and thinking, and they just happen to have been captured as a tool of theater and have since been transformed into merely performance; believe that the adult learning community may also claim these as their own.

Future Needs
1. In terms of the steps that I can take, I see a greatest need in:
a. helping adult learners and teachers to find the potential of using the theater arts as a part of their learning situation. This might take the form of a workshop that can be introduced to adult learning communities and introduces basic concepts of the theater arts to adult learning groups: making the connection directly from the theater arts to teaching in the adult learning world, from the point of view of applied theater in education.
b. finding elements of existing adult education environments that are already working toward social change and help to form a collaboration between them in this particular area, such as an ongoing practice group for discovering new ways to use theater within their own contexts - these could include centers for adult/continuing education, community activist groups, or neighborhood groups.

Initial Assumptions and Perspectives
• three major elements: theater arts, adult education, social change
• meanings of each
• main idea

Research findings and Activities
- theater and social change Africa and Latin America
- theater in social change in the U.S. is often more narrow
- theater arts may be introduced as a tool in teacher education

New Ideas
- subversive view of "adult education"
- "methodologies of theater arts" are actually more fundamental aspects of human behavior and thinking

Future Needs
- workshop
- adult ed. ongoing practice group

Questions
- do you see other ways that this idea is relevant in your own teaching/learning situations?
- as an adult, what do you want in your own learning situations to make them more enjoyable?

Presentation, Part 2
Overview of Project and Initial Assumptions
- neglect as an adult learner
- usually, mention of "education" means primary/ secondary/ university, and even adult education usually means professional skills development or personal life enhancement
- experience in adult ed, theater, social change led me to feel that there was a relationship between these that was unfulfilled
- relationship centers on the idea that change can happen through learning at a community level as well as an individual one, and that's where I needed to focus my attention

New Directions
- after my research, I've found so far that there well-established relationship between theater and social change (forum theater)
- also, there is an emerging relationship between the course of adult education and social change - in my opinion, the pioneers of

adult education are advocating a focus on learning that targets how we can address social issues, and I think that's the right track
• greatest need: stronger relationship between adult. ed and theater —this is what I think will provide a medium to return the natural joy and fun of learning, because using theater provides a lot of powerful tools for ideas like taking on alternative points of view, helping us to find common understanding of social issues, and find common ground with others in the course of problem-solving
• right now, I think this relationship exists but seemed to be owned by people experienced in theater who bring activities to education, but this focuses much on children; I think the direction of my work needs to be to work with those in adult learning to understand how these tools can be available to them in a long term process, and find ways that adult learners and teachers can take ownership of them in such a way that they support social change and collaboration
• extract the "generic" parts of theater
• turn the notion of adult education "on its head"

Questions/Clarifications
• 1-minute activity - want a starting point for a dialogue about becoming aware of how we make judgments about others and what we think they want
• Discussion of the learning group
- one initial idea is that a kind of ongoing support group for those in adult education - learners and teachers - a way to experiment with activities such as this and find ways to both tie them to helping support social change as well as find practical ways to apply them in the learning setting/classroom
- pretend that you are all part of the adult learning community, and I invited you to join this support group; I want to know: what would cause you to come in the first place?
- how would the group meet or communicate on an ongoing basis?
- what would make you feel comfortable about participating - bringing ideas for activities, sharing your experiences, etc.?
- in situations where you participate in any kind of ongoing activity, what causes you to keep going back?

Narrative Outline

Governing Question: What are the steps that I can take to engage the adult learning communities in using the principles of theater arts to prepare them to create social change?

1. In my own experience, I have come to support fundamental principles of adult education as a means of achieving social change, although I currently find this field, particularly in North American culture, to be primarily focused on professional skills development instead. My involvement as an adult education teacher, administrator, and student has demonstrated that learning for social change seems to be rarely considered in the needs of curriculum, classrooms, and lifelong learning settings.

2. Social change involves learning in which people can collectively use their knowledge to collaboratively improve the conditions of their social environment, which affects all members of a community.

3. Traditional learning and teaching methods are insufficient for preparing adult learners for social change because they often imply a didactic style of transfer of subject-level information in a unidirectional style from teacher to student. In the learning toward social change, other principles must be considered which account for the existing experience of adults, their ability to organize their collective knowledge and understand each other, and the ability of adults to work together and take over ownership of the direction of their learning and the resulting action.

4. Through my more recent experience in theater-based learning experiences, I have found that the fundamental tools of theater seem applicable to adult learning. These are the tools that allow for the reflection of and experimentation with the core elements of human behavior in collaborative situations, such as empathy, point-

of-view, interpersonal interaction, and dialogue. Also, they represent an enjoyable way to learn because they use a very natural concept of "character" in learning - the ability to discover and use one's "alternative selves" as a way to let go of personal inhibitions, take a perspective of another person, and envision a new reality in which social issues are changed.

5. One step that I can take is to develop an idea for ways to engage adult education communities to understand these tools. Because I view it to be critically important that members of this community experience these first-hand, I will consider the way that a "theater for social change" ongoing learning group could be formed and supported, including how to define the structure of the group, how to engage adult educators to attend, participate in, and support the group, and how to introduce the tools of theater to the group in a way that allows the participants to associate them most effectively with the teaching of social change in their own areas.

6. Another step that I can take is to define more specifically the ways in which the methods of theater can be used directly to teach social change. This can take the form of a series of examples and suggested applications that help those in adult education to use the theater methods most relevant to social change. These applications may serve as a foundation of educational curriculum, teaching methodologies, and in the way that the educational environment is set up.

Work In Progress for a Project on Engaging Adult Learning Communities in Using The Principles of Theater Arts to Prepare Them to Create Social Change, Phase H

Final Report

(excerpt - Introduction only)
Title: "Recapturing the Joy of Adult Education Through a Theater Arts Perspective of Learning Toward a Renewed Purpose of Social Change"

A Revolution in Fun

Imagine yourself sitting in a classroom, waiting patiently for a lecture to finish while the minutes tick along on the clock. You have been paying attention throughout the class, and you have dutifully taken notes and raised your hand to answer a question and make a comment or two. You feel great because you managed to stay alert enough throughout the class to scribble down some notes, and you think that that you understand today's topic. Class is almost over, and already, your thoughts are beginning to turn toward the trip home. There is bound to be a lot of traffic today, and you are supposed to stop by the grocery store...what was it that you needed to pick up? You'll probably remember later. You hope that it doesn't snow again tomorrow—how many times have you shoveled the sidewalk this month?

"See you next week."

The instructor's voice trails off as just manage to return your attention back to the classroom. At least you heard those most important last words, you think to yourself, as you spring up from your chair and direct your eyes and body toward the door as you move. Yes! It's your favorite time of day and finally this last class is over and you get your freedom back. Until tomorrow, at least.

This is not the way that adult education is supposed to work.

Rather than feeling the rush of relief as we leave the classroom, shouldn't we feel at least the slightest twinge of disappointment? Why can't our learning experiences enthrall us and allow us to recapture the joy that we once felt so easily? There is a natural sense of fun in learning that involves exploring our curiosities, playing with new ideas, discovering humor in our own knowledge (or lack thereof), and give ourselves and others permission to try, fail, succeed, become confused, and become enlightened—often? Children seem to "own" this sense of fun, which is then systematically stripped away as we move toward adulthood. The secret of adult education, though, is that enjoyment in learning actually belongs to everyone—learners of all ages, and this represents a gap between the way that adult education works today and the way that it could work. Make no mistake though—the joy of learning is not a "game" or just a way to make us "feel good." As adults, we must both once again accept this joy while channeling our learning toward a purpose that might give us something more than just a credential, a job, a promotion, or a new hobby..."

Work In Progress for a Project on Engaging Adult Learning Communities in Using The Principles of Theater Arts to Prepare Them to Create Social Change, Phase I

With respect to the goal of Phase I: "I have facilitated new avenues of classroom, workplace, and public participation," let me point to:

• My **Action Research** project. (This is not a direct illustration of Engagement with Others around "Recapturing the Joy of Adult Education Through a Theater Arts Perspective of Learning," but it shows the way my work actually unfolded.)

• The CCT Network (http://cct.wikispaces.umb.edu/CCT Network) that I helped to initiate in 2008 and have since co-organized. The Network's monthly events and online community aim to:

- organize, in a sustainable fashion, personal and professional development, community building, and educational-innovation activities beyond the formal program of studies in Critical and Creative Thinking;
- supplement students' education through the involvement of alums; and
- continue alums' education by their involvement in the education of students and each other.

Work In Progress for a Project on Engaging Adult Learning Communities in Using The Principles of Theater Arts to Prepare Them to Create Social Change, Phase J

Self-Assessment, at the End

Instructions

Self-assessment with respect to two sets of goals:
  I. **Phases of Research and Engagement**; and
  II. **Reflective Practitioner Goals**, including taking initiative in or through relationships
In the **Plus-Delta** mode, you should describe two things for each goal:
• one that reflects what you have achieved well related to this goal, and
• one you have struggled with or need more help on or want to work further on.
(Even though you may have many examples for some items, one is enough.)

I. "MY SUBMISSION SHOWS THAT..."

A. I can convey who I want to influence or affect concerning what (Subject, Audience, Purpose).

<u>Did well</u>: I was able to converge onto my ideas fairly quickly and found a true personal interest and passion about my topic that I believe I was able to convey to others with sincerity through the course of the project.

<u>To be improved</u>: I would like to continue exploring how my topic can connect in more personal ways to others, and I would like to able to demonstrate the enjoyment of using theater in education for social change in more active ways.

B. I know what others have done before, either in the form of writing or action, that informs and connects with my project, and I know what others are doing now.

<u>Did well</u>: I was able to identify the areas of the work of Augusto Boal that applied to my topic and found that other independent threads often connected to that as a foundation.

To be improved: I still would like to know more about other adult education practitioners who might already share my ideas but who are not also formal theater practitioners - I have found fewer people of this type so far.

C. I have teased out my vision, so as to expand my view of issues associated with the project, expose possible new directions, clarify direction/scope within the larger set of issues, and decide the most important direction.

Did well: My idea-mapping allowed a major breakthrough to happen as it helped me to prioritize the relationship between theater, education, and social change and helped me to choose the scope of my research in a more confident way.

To be improved: Because I am interested in so many areas, it was easy throughout my research to follow new threads, meaning that I needed to constantly step back from my work and verify that I was using my time effectively.

D. I have identified the premises and propositions that my project depends on, and can state counter-propositions. I have taken stock of the thinking and research I need to do to counter those counter-propositions or to revise my own propositions.

Did well: I was able to use information from my initial informants as well as from published research to understand counter-propositions, which I believe added a more grounded element to them and therefore helped me to think about them in practical ways.

To be improved: I feel in some ways that my counter-counter-propositions in writing are still limited in that they may not address deeper feelings of hesitation of adult learners to engage in any kind of "theater", so I realize that a part of my research is to appreciate the need for ongoing, long-term conversations with people as well as simply making a logical argument.

E. I have clear objectives with respect to product, both written and practice, and process, including personal development as a reflective practitioner. I have arranged my work in a sequence (with realistic deadlines) to realize these objectives.

<u>Did well</u>: I was able to develop a strategy which allowed me to start to limit the expanse of my research and finally decide to address specific areas within my interests, so this greatly improved my timeline of work and kept it in to a realistic form.

<u>To be improved</u>: As I focused on my final conclusions in the later part of the research, I sometimes neglected some of the smaller organizational elements that might have helped me consider my work in smaller chunks.

F. I have gained direct information, models, and experience not readily available from other sources.

<u>Did well</u>: I was able to speak with several people involved in areas within my research as well as observe a practical application.

<u>To be improved</u>: All of my interviews and informants suggested additional threads of inquiry, and it will be an ongoing process to follow them as this continues to expand.

G. I have clarified the overall progression or argument underlying my research and the written reports.

<u>Did well</u>: I was able to gain insight about my presentation from my practice presentation, and this prompted me to consider new ideas about my final project.

<u>To be improved</u>: I would like to continue to develop group activities that could be used in future presentations or situations to more specifically demonstrate how theater concepts relate to social change.

H. My writing and other products Grab the attention of the readers or audience, Orient them, move them along in Steps, so they appreciate the Position I've led them to.

<u>Did well</u>: Because of my ranges of ideas, I felt that I was able to explore several in my writing while also find a writing organization that made sense.

<u>To be improved</u>: I would like to continue to improve the way that I utilize other members of the class and become partners in our writing and research efforts.

I. I have facilitated new avenues of classroom, workplace, and public participation.

<u>Did well</u>: I believe that my personal enthusiasm for my topic and the flexibility of it allows for numerous opportunities for participation and even depends upon it. so I look forward to continuing how that may work.

<u>To be improved</u>: I would like to continue to improve my own abilities as a facilitator of groups and gain some practical experience.

J. To feed into my future learning and other work, I have taken stock of what has been working well and what needs changing.

<u>Did well</u>: I was able to discipline myself fairly well throughout the research process and never felt that I was behind according to the progress that I intended to make.

<u>To be improved</u>: It took me a while to understand my pockets of time during a given week due to a completely new and complex schedule relative to my classes and work experiences. I need to find a better way to examine this in the future.

II. DEVELOPING AS A REFLECTIVE PRACTITIONER, INCLUDING TAKING INITIATIVE IN AND THROUGH RELATIONSHIPS

1. I have integrated knowledge and perspectives from CCT (Critical and Creative Thinking graduate program, University of Massachusetts Boston) and other courses into my own inquiry and engagement in social or educational change.

<u>Did well</u>: I feel that my recent CCT experience had already started me to be much more aware of relinquishing my old "labels" for myself, and that encouraged me through this course to start to

consider ideas and interests that I did not accept before.

To be improved: I would like to make sure to engage in dialogue with more of the CCT community – even though I have attended department events, I would like to appreciate the work of other students even more.

2. I have also integrated into my own inquiry and engagement the processes, experiences, and struggles of previous courses.

Did well: I found that I was much more able to allow myself to be assisted by others in my inquiry compared to past experiences, in which I spent more time in independent study and research.

To be improved: Through the Dialogue course this winter, I would like to pay particular attention to use of dialogue in groups and need to think of this as another key layer to my current research.

3. I have developed efficient ways to organize my time, research materials, computer access, bibliographies...

Did well: It arose early in the course that my "in-between" times might be utilized more effective, such as when I am traveling between places or while I am waiting for class to begin, etc. I feel that I have trained myself to actually plan to think as well as finish tasks during certain times, and I have never before really organized my time to actually carve out space for merely thinking.

To be improved: Because of my limited physical space for organizing class materials, I would like to find a new system for maintaining my books, articles, notebooks, and other items. I need to think more about "containers" for my research that might take a different form other than bookshelves.

4. I have experimented with new tools and experiences, even if not every one became part of my toolkit as a learner, teacher/facilitator of others, and reflective practitioner.

Did well: I feel that the experiences of both freewriting and writing feedback were particularly powerful to me, since the freewriting allows me to dedicate time to my inner dialogue and allow it to make connections between ideas and then see them visually on a page. I appreciate the idea of writing feedback styles because I observe that allowing a point of view in feedback really helps me to view my writing in terms of intentions and impact on others rather than simply getting out what I want to say.

To be improved: In our use of Post-it activities, I found this to be useful but feel that I didn't take advantage of Post-its enough independently in my own work. I think this is necessary because I do tend to write easily and extensively, but the Post-it activities help me to condense my language and find essence more easily.

5. I have paid attention to the emotional dimensions of undertaking my own project but have found ways to clear away distractions from other sources (present & past) and not get blocked, turning apparent obstacles into opportunities to move into unfamiliar or uncomfortable territory.

Did well: I have been able to expose the emotional impact of my research to friends, family, and classmates much more than I have done in the past, and for me this is an important breakthrough because I have been able to focus on my accomplishments when I have gotten lost in my "to-do" list, and this has actually helped me to feel more comfortable about taking care of high-priority items first without worrying about "everything else."

To be improved: I found that I did still tend to consider large elements of my project and become hesitant to address them all at once, so I need to become better at simply starting the first short steps of a new assignment or task right away after I am ready for them, rather than feeling that I need to reflect on the meaning first. In other words, I would like to improve on getting physically involved in a piece of work before I really know what I am doing.

6. I have developed peer and other horizontal relationships. I have sought support and advice from peers, and have given support and advice to them when asked for.

Did well: I have found that I have been able to share my work and ideas with other peers outside of the context of class, even with those not taking the course. I have found that it has become much easier for me to ask someone, "what do you think?" and frame it in a way that indicates that I am not just looking for approval but challenges to help me. In this sense, my style of communication in seeking support from peers has improved.

<u>To be improved</u>: I would like to continue to find new ways to engage others in dialogue about our directions and interests, particularly with respect to CCT as a whole. I feel that I know many peers on the level of classwork but would like to continue to establish peer relationships that persist more cohesively between classes as well as within a single class.

7. I have taken the lead, not dragged my feet, in dialogue with my instructor and other readers. I didn't wait for the them to tell me how to solve an expository problem, what must be read and covered in the literature, or what was meant by some comment I didn't understand. I didn't put off giving my writing to my instructor and other readers or avoid talking to them because I thought that they didn't see things the same way as I do.

<u>Did well</u>: I feel that I really took advantage of the suggested assignment dates for the course by making them a self-imposed requirement, and this gave me a way to restrict my work so that I felt that I had to finish milestones on-time. Also, I came to realize more and more that comments from instructors and peers were not necessarily meant to be taken as literal action items, but instead could be filtered back through my own ideas, allowing me to more easily accept comments from others such that I was then actually making them my own.

<u>To be improved</u>: Because I consider an important element of my research to be encouraging others to participate in some of my ideas, I need to spend more time and thought considering the fact that others don't see things my way, and that I am not really trying to convince others but instead am trying to invite others to explore these ideas with me.

8. I have revised seriously, which involved responding to the comments of others. I came to see this not as bowing down to the views of others, but taking them in and working them into my own reflective inquiry until I could convey more powerfully to others what I'm about (which may have changed as a result of the reflective inquiry).

Did well: As mentioned above, I have become more successful at accepting comments from the point of view of making them my own. Additionally, I feel that I have been allow my own enthusiasm to come out more in my presentation of ideas verbally and in writing.

To be improved: I would like to find creative ways to prompt additionally feedback, since I would have liked even more from peers. Because of the limits of the time of others, I would like to both find alternative ways to know the views of others and also allow myself more opportunities to use methodological believing in my own daily work.

9. I have inquired and negotiated about formal standards, but gone on to develop and internalize my own criteria for doing work—criteria other than jumping through hoops set by the instructor so I get a good grade.

Did well: I feel that as the course progressed, I was able to think much more about creating a foundation of work that could be sustained outside the course and after it was over. This helped me to take attention off of criteria and on to making sure that I was making sense to myself and actually was creating work that I could stand behind with confidence.

To be improved: This particular issue may always be a challenge for me, because even more so than with grades and evaluations, it has been important to me to feel that I have showed my best work to others. I believe that if I can more naturally and immediate observe coursework and the CCT program as a process that happens to result in certain products, then I can relieve myself of being concerned with actually creating the products and understand how well I am utilizing the process.

10. I have approached this course as a work-in-progress. Instead of harboring criticisms to submit after the fact, I have found opportunities to affirm what is working well the course and suggest directions for further development.

<u>Did well</u>: Most of all, I feel that this course has represented a starting point of future work, so I have been able to find ways to "forgive" myself for unexplored areas and have found through that realization that I do now possess knowledge and skills in my area of interest that might actually be able to benefit others as well as my own continued work.

<u>To be improved</u>: Because my work involves collaboration and experimentation with others, I would like to make sure to keep my momentum going and notice when I come across opportunities to have personal and direct involvement in areas where my interests appear. This means actively seeking out opportunities and making sure to continue to discuss my work in CCT with people outside of the program.

ILLUSTRATION of CYCLES and EPICYCLES

Development of an Action Research Project on Collaborative Play by Teachers in Curriculum Planning

This case illustrates the **Cycles and Epicycles of Action Research** as it was experienced by someone learning to use the framework. The illustrations are intended to draw readers into the *process*. The case does not cut to the chase and describe some outstanding final outcome as if that would convince readers that the framework works.

Background and Motivation

When I first started this project, I had been working at a local community center as the multimedia instructor at a preschool/afterschool program, responsible for developing curriculum that integrated core subjects (reading literacy, number and math skills, science and nature, social skills, and cultural awareness) with technology resources such as computer software, web-based learning materials, and digital photo/video equipment. Each student was part of one of five groups, where groups 1-4 were preschool levels of representing ages 2.9 - 6 years old, and group 5 was an afterschool level representing ages 6 - 12. Before my arrival, no such multimedia instruction was included in the curriculum.

When I first arrived, I noticed that each of the 5 groups was somewhat independent of the other - one or two head teachers were responsible for a given group, and other than some very general monthly themes that were supposed to span across curriculum, teachers were generally independent in terms of how they planned activities for the students and were able to focus on the needs of the students in their own group. When a multimedia component was developed, I realized that my role was initially perceived as yet another independent grouping, that is, toward a learning experience that was relatively isolated from what the groups were doing in their group classrooms. At the same time, I saw that my responsibility was to introduce the tools of technology in a new way in support of what was already being done in the classrooms with the core subjects, not simply to teach "computers for computers' sake." This meant that my own teaching, lesson plans, and curriculum would need to use these technology resources as a means to another end - particularly school readiness (for the preschool groups) and reinforcement of school lessons and opportunities for creative expression (for the afterschool group).

Very quickly, I found that the idea of cross-group planning had room for expansion, and started to consider how the teacher planning process might be developed to create a culture of greater collaboration in planning and do so in a way that was more enjoyable for teachers rather than seem like another administrative meeting for a group of teachers who were otherwise faced with all of the demands of supervising and teaching young children. While I considered that the greatest need would involve the preschool groups, I also considered that I might like to pursue this idea to some extent with the afterschool group as well.

Because of my long-term interest and perspectives on adult education, I finally decided that my own action research might involve the idea of the use of play in the teacher planning process. How could play be used to develop integrated lesson plans that represented the experience and needs of multiple teachers? What kinds of play would be acceptable to adult teachers in a formal setting of needing to decide and document classroom lessons and curriculum? How might the use of play in planning mirror the learning style and environment of the youth classroom? Within a short period of time in the action research process, I realized that I needed to settle upon a slightly more modest question, as those above contained a large assumption that play would already be a natural part of the planning process. Because of this, I started with

ILLUSTRATIONS

process with an initial question of "In what ways might collaborative play be introduced into the teacher planning process?" I would focus on getting play to happen at all and leave its ultimate effect as a later concern. Could my personal actions, attitudes, and behavior translate into actually using some form of collaborative play in teacher planning, to what extent might this happen, and what forms of play might be manifested through this process?

Development of an Action Research Project on Collaborative Play by Teachers in Curriculum Planning

Novice Reflection

Notes: At this stage in the course, I was coming to understand two particular aspects of the action research cycle. First, after relating the main stages of action research to my own work, I was starting to get insight into the idea of the process as a cycle - that is, I was able to let go of planning the entire scope of my project, realizing that I would need to evaluate the results of initial action plans in any case and therefore have future chances to revise - I did not need to think of my work with a single, monolithic result of high-level change. Rather, my planning now could aim to develop my actions as a collection of small steps rather than large ones. Second, I had just started to see far ahead enough to know that collaboration would become a part of my process in the form of comments and discussion with classmates. This understanding helped to motivate me to find small ways to test and explore my ideas about using play in the collaborative curriculum planning process - apart from insights that might directly help my own action research, the anticipation of collaborating with classmates nudged me to start to take action in my workplace, so that at the least I would have something substantive to share by the time I arrived at the class each week.

At this point in my CCT career, I feel that I have enough experience with the style of the program to have become much more comfortable and certainly even excited about our class sessions. I have developed a sort of mantra in my mind in preparation for any class session, consisting of the two following expectations:
• it's perfectly ok to spend a little time in class not yet completely understanding what is happening or why what is happening is important
• I trust that whatever does happen in class and as the result of the

class will somehow expose more potential for making use of my experience as fully as possible

Both of these expectations were met during my first experience with my novice exposure to Action Research through exploring the issue of refreshments and snacks. [PT: Refreshments and snacks are a feature of all CCT courses, which meet for 2.5 hours in the evening. The activity JS refers to was designed to give students a quick first look at the whole Cycles and Epicycles framework for Action Research on a situation they were all familiar with, namely, arranging "break time and provision of class refreshments in a way that enhances the educational experience."] At a few moments during our first two class sessions, I found myself cringing during a few times when another student expressed some anxiety about the specifics of an assignment in terms of "what has to be done" in terms of meeting the official requirements, such as the length of a paper. When I reflected on why such questions from others cause me to be a little uncomfortable, I found that my feelings stem from my own motivation to get past such logistical details as quickly as possible so that I can focus my attention to thinking about how to make the work as personally meaningful as possible.

A connection seemed to form between this realization and to some of the initial illustrations and descriptions of the action research process and to Professor Taylor's explanations of the cycles and epicycles. Through our activity, I have started to see how our treatment of the refreshments issue provided an opening for me to more greatly explore why and how certain issues are most important to me. This did not mean getting things to be the way that I wanted, but it did have something to do with permitting myself to pay greater attention to my own motivations and wants during the process itself. Several times, I found myself doing what Schmuck referred to as "catching myself in the act of behaving", which mostly occurred in the form of remembering past experiences with refreshments in previous class situations, most particularly in the ways that I thought our process for refreshments might have been better. I "caught myself" by noticing that my responses and questions in many ways reflected memories of past cases of handing refreshments. Had I not noticed this, I don't believe that I would have then considered that my level of satisfaction about the refreshments was based on the more deep-seeded value of inclusion and sharing among class members (rather than nutrition, scheduling, or how to distribute responsibility).

As far as Schmuck also describes Action Research as involving what the researcher is doing personally and the way that the cycles are truly continuous by reflecting, planning, and evaluating change, I'm also starting to relate the compressed action research to my overall interests in adult learning. One idea for future exploration is my underlying motivation to improve my own lifelong learning because of the disappointment that I feel about the way that the potential of my formal childhood schooling was never met. In a way, many of the actions that I take now and perspectives of learning may be manifestations of me reacting to this unresolved issue of the past. Through the process of considering refreshments, the obvious thought that came to mind was that the process was helping to strip away more generic issues to explore the issues of refreshments with finer levels of granularity. The less obvious thought that emerged later was the idea that the process was also stripping away my own more generic interest in 'knowledge' to uncover the finer layers of my *personal interest* in the issue. Schmuck discusses the levels of concern in research in which one focuses on self, then on others, then on results, and our activity reminds me that it is all too easy for me to skip directly to the focus on others.

Finally, the focus of our Action Research on improvement rather than correctness has helped me to become more inspired about how my thoughts might develop in my current work situation in which I develop educational resources and classroom activities for a preschool and afterschool program. Although my primary interest is in adult learning, I had decided to spend the current school year working in childhood education, thinking that it would inspire some insight about what it means to enjoy learning and feel free about one's natural curiosities and willingness to experiment in learning. In this work so far, there is constant planning of new ways to engage the students and evaluate and then reflect upon the results. Admittedly, I have occasionally worked through this process with the intention that I could eventually "get it right" and therefore not need to repeat the cycle, perhaps even seeming to indicate that I had failed at times. Through our initial classwork so far, I have started to change my mind and trust that this pattern is not only expected but a very positive indication that progress can happen in rewarding ways without concern for being "finished."

Development of an Action Research Project on Collaborative Play by Teachers in Curriculum Planning

Paragraph Overview

I would like to continue my ongoing exploration of adult learning and what it means for learners to include a greater sense of fun and play throughout the process. An emerging goal of this examination is to more clearly understand how actions that I take contribute to making a group learning opportunity more enjoyable and engaging others in play along with me. For an action research plan, I would like to consider the way that I approach my own behavior around personal learning opportunities with respect to the following "Core Actions":

1. what actions I take to prepare myself for the upcoming learning opportunity: how can I use play to prepare for the learning opportunity?
2. what actions I take during the learning opportunity: how can I play while I'm actually involved in learning discussion and activities?
3. what actions I take to build upon the learning opportunity after it is over: how can I play during my reflection of the recent learning experience?

Although I am involved in a number of adult learning situations, I have found that one may be particularly useful as a reference point in thinking about collaborative play. In my work at a youth center, my role is to assist lead teachers by developing educational materials and activities for preschool (ages 3-5) and afterschool (ages 6-12) students. Specifically, I help the teachers to integrate multimedia and information technology into their lessons, since I am knowledgeable in that area, and the teachers are knowledgeable of the learning topics and goals of the students, and we must share and combine our knowledge to create activities that utilize both. I would like to explore in what ways I might define the Core Actions such that our planning interactions are improved, as these do not typically involve collaborative play.

Evaluation might include comparing a number of variables observed between the planning interactions that do and do not use collaborative play. These include the level of enjoyment experienced by myself and the teachers, whether or not humor is embraced into the planning process in a new way, whether or not teachers agree to engage in collaborative play, whether or not planned actions for collaborative play actually happened and why, whether or not the later learning experiences of the students were enhanced by through activities that were conceived through planning that used collaborative play, and whether or not my own and the teachers' understandings of each other's areas of expertise were deepened through the experience of collaborative play. Iterations through the action research process should then shape my "Personal Engagement Plan" - a practical recipe that I could use to guide myself into the actions that make the learning opportunity more playful for myself and others before, during, and after it takes place. Developing my constituency would then include the other teachers with whom I was working, administrators/directors of the center, the students who would eventually be influenced by the results of the lesson planning, and other educational supporters who might suggest ways of play that would enhance the process.

Development of an Action Research Project on Collaborative Play by Teachers in Curriculum Planning

KAQF

What do we **K**now?
Action: What could people do on the basis of this knowledge?
Questions for Inquiry: What more do we need to know - in order to clarify what people could do or to revise/refine knowledge?
How to **F**ind this out?

K—Children naturally engage in play in their learning
-Play involves deviating from the direct path from question to answer and requires experimenting, imagining, and having fun
A—Adults may take a point of view in learning that embraces curiosity, naiveté, and open-minded exploration
-Seek out learning opportunities that are flexibly structured and involve understanding of ideas beyond just acquisition of skill
Q—What has other research/experience shown about how to embrace play in learning experiences?
F—Ask adults about which learning experiences they have found to be fun (and recall personal examples)
-Research examples of successful play in learning settings

K—Using play in learning may help relieve tension about "being wrong" or "knowing the answer already."
A—Play can be used at the beginning of a learning situation to help learners become more comfortable with each other and establish a safe, nonjudgmental environment.
-Learning situation can be explicitly structured as a forum of encouraging experimentation and even failure.
Q—In what ways does collaborative play improve learning? How does play influence the understanding that is sought in learning experiences?
F—Describe ways that collaborative play might be used and test in various learning situations.
-Review studies of types of play in learning.
-Reflect upon and keep a record of new understanding that I gain in the course of play.

K—I have not frequently considered how direct actions that I take individually affect the collaborative play of learning.
-The actions that I take might actually influence the collaboration of the group in learning - this is not wholly determined by the "teacher" or the interpersonal dynamics of the group.
A—Observe actions that I take before, during, and after learning experiences.
-Create a specific plan to take action before, during, and after learning.
-Develop a learning environment that is student-, rather than teacher-, driven.
-In any learning experience, take on the role of "teacher" myself and guide others to engage in collaborative play.
Q—How do the individual actions that I take influence the collaborative play of the group?
F—Create a plan to take certain types of actions before, during, and after learning.
-Seek experiences in everyday life in which no "teacher" is defined and treat them as a "bona fide" learning opportunity.
-In my own role as a teacher or student, expose my intentions to play and make my experiments transparent, and observe reactions of myself and others.

K—Factors beyond my personal control may influence the success of my learning.
-Adults in learning situations may not agree to collaborate or engage in play.
A—Set small-scale learning goals for play.
-Allow the meaning of "collaborative play" to be understood broadly and include many types of play.
QWhat might prevent me from taking planned actions in establishing collaborative play?
F—Record and observe how and why planned actions did not get done.
-Ask others to review my planned actions and provide explicit support or clarify why my actions may not be realistic.

K—Play relates to fun in learning and might be observed through facial expressions, laughter, or direct verbal communication.
-Collaborative play means that multiple learners are engaged in the same activity of play.
A—Develop fun learning activities that are designed to be inclusive of all learners in a group.

-Notice that I am enjoying my learning through metacognitive reflection of my learning while it is happening.

Q—What do I need to observe in adult learning situations to determine when collaborative play is actually happening?

F—Consider the range of emotions and responses that I express during a learning experience.

-Note instances in which adult learners are engaged with each other how their specific actions relate to their ways of communicating/involving others.

K—There are organizing groups who already use the notion of play in learning.

-Several personal colleagues already express openness for play, including children in my afterschool/preschool and the CCT community.

A—Use my own teaching experiences (preschool) and student experiences (CCT program) to seek support and permission in play activities.

Q—Who are my potential allies, partners, or assistants in the course of designing, implementing, participating, and observing play?

F—Research groups/workshops that seek to provide practice/training in play in learning.

-Explicitly define different roles that supporters might take in play - observer, participant, idea-generator, etc.

K—Theater principles help people to take on behaviors of other people with foreign/unfamiliar points of view.

-Theater principles help people to develop/imagine conceptual realities that are not as obvious to the everyday authentic self (empathy).

-Theater involves a type of "game" of agreement between actors to temporarily accept the existence of a common fantasy situation.

A—Take theater classes to explore the notions of character, dialogue, and empathy.

-Engage in role-play.

-Invent ways of perceiving through another's point of view and try them out during learning.

Q—What specific principles of the theater perspective might relate to allowing play to happen?

F—Create a Personal Action Plan that utilized theater exercises to prepare me for upcoming collaborative learning situations.

-Use theater methodologies to play with ideas or find humor in learning content; employ these during the learning experiences; observe the results.

-Discuss and explore options with others already using integrated theater/education concepts.

K—Lifelong learning may involve finding specific learning opportunities but also taking an attitude of recognizing long-term learning goals and needs.

-Collaborative play may encourage learners to take a long-term view of learning by relieving the "chore" of education.

A—Develop a long-term, continuous plan for what learning experiences one wishes to have.

-Find ways to focus on the play of learning with others primarily while considering learning outcome of be secondary at times.

Q—How does collaborative play support ongoing, lifelong learning?

F—Commit to developing a cycle of planning, implementing, and observing in my own learning.

-Ask other adult learners to reflect upon their lifelong learning wishes.

-Along with allies, develop a learner's group for developing and experimenting with collaborative learning ideas.

Development of an Action Research Project on Collaborative Play by Teachers in Curriculum Planning

Evaluation Clock

Notes on changes made from version 1 to version 2: while version 1 considered a scenario where some "naïve" participants were not told that research was happening, this version has been modified to allow that all participants are able to be aware of the project. This time, there are "direct" participants who are actively taking action to develop the use of collaborative play in teacher planning meetings, "indirect" participants who are part of the planning group but are not asked to take such actions, and "observers" who are not part of the planning group but openly observe the process and take notes that will be used for evaluating the results.

0a. The intervention whose effect or effectiveness needs to be evaluated is...

The practice involves taking action that will introduce the use of collaborative play in teacher planning in order to better prepare teachers to create more effective lesson plans and activities for students. My suggestion is that in situations when teachers have an opportunity to work together to create lesson plans and are structured to do so anyway, they use collaborative play as a methodology to help them 1) learn from each other's strengths and teaching styles, 2) develop lesson plans and activities that are creative in the sense that they involve combining ideas of diverse practitioners that might not be considered by one teacher doing own planning in isolation, and 3) they allow lesson plans and activities to be developed which exhibit greater continuity across different classes, since the plans would be reflective of multiple teachers and the process of creating them would allow teachers to become more aware of each other's goals and needs, which could help support consistent environments for students between different classrooms.

0b. Interest or concern in the effect/iveness of the change arises because...

In many "collaborative" teacher planning meetings, I have noticed that this planning very often manifests in the form of a discussion, involving a cycle of brainstorming, evaluation, and decision, where the teachers themselves do not participate in direct experimentation but instead theorize "best practices" and then commit to lesson plans without further inquiry. Particularly in many of my past teaching situations, I feel that use of collaborative play would have helped me to learn and reflect more about what I was actually doing while allowing the practical work to get done.

1a. The group or person(s) that sponsor the evaluation of the intervention are...

I am the main sponsor within my own environment, which is too small for a statistically significant sample, but within a larger institution, the administrators/directors might be the main sponsors as they seek to improve the collaboration of teachers in the school or center.

1b. The people they seek to influence with the results are...

I seek to influence primarily the other teachers in my school environment (in my specific case, this might be the team of teachers responsible for planning toward youth education). A secondary influence would ideally occur with the students, who are the beneficiaries of the teachers who do use collaborative play.

1c. The actions or decisions or policies those people might improve or affirm concern...

The teachers might improve or affirm the need for scheduled and organized planning, the role of facilitation in teacher planning, and the allowance for developing ideas that need not always be fully worked out at the end of a specific planning session.

2a. General Question: The comparison needed to evaluate the effectiveness of the change is between two (or more) situations, namely a. a comparison of...

The two situations being compared are the teacher planning sessions in which no member of the group takes particular interest in collaborative play, and those sessions in which at least one person does take interest in collaborative play and attempts to integrate it into the planning approach.

b. with respect to differences in the general area of.....

In the latter situation in which some planning group members do advocate use of collaborative play, the main action to be considered, planned, and evaluated is the taking of steps that encourage collaborative play to happen. For example with my specific situation, I would consider what actions would I need to take before, during, and after teacher planning with certain groups, and I would not take such actions with the "control" groups. As well as the actual actions taken by teachers, another difference would be that some outside person or party would be present to observe the interactions of the teachers during planning and note observations that could be used to help the evaluation of collaborative play integration.

3. Specific observables: To undertake that comparison, the effects of the intervention will be assessed by looking at the following specific variable(s) in the two (or more) situations...

Across a large number of teacher planning groups, "control" groups would go on as always, and "treatment" groups would be the ones to utilize collaborative play. Within the treatment group, there would be "direct participants" who are actively involved in introducing collaborative play into the planning sessions, and then

ILLUSTRATIONS

"indirect participants" who do not specifically plan for collaborative play. The direct participants would adhere to a set of common "collaborative play" actions that they would take before, during, and after teacher planning, and they would not necessarily reveal that they are doing to others in the whole group. At first, these collaborative actions might be developed in a common form by those actually implementing them, although it seems likely that the flexibility would be need to be allowed for them to evolve. The "before" and "after" actions would help the direct participant him- or herself prepare for and reflect upon collaborative play individually, and the "during" actions would involve more direct collaborative play while actually engaged in the teacher planning. Alternately, the treatment group might contain all direct participants and no indirect participants, meaning that the entire process would be transparent to all involved, and everyone would be taking the actions to invoke play. This might necessitate forming groups that don't typically meet with each other for planning. In more "natural" planning groups, teachers in a same grade level or teaching a similar subject might typically meet, and in these cases, it might be realistic that only certain members of the group are open to acting as direct participants.

Variables would include the following:
1) The number of planned actions that were either taken or not taken by the direct participants
2) The expressions of acceptance or resistance made in response to the collaborative play actions "during" the teacher planning (as made by the indirect participants) in a planning group
3) Over time, the number of instances when indirect participants start to introduce collaborative play approaches themselves
4) Time spent and actions taken during periods of collaborative play, i.e., when experimentation of proposed learning activities is happening between teachers such that they are expressing enjoyment and finding freedom to explicitly and personally try the activities without expectation of specific results.

4. The methods to be used to produce observations or measurements of those variables are...(survey, questionnaire, etc.)

Methods would require that third-party observers take notes during teacher planning meetings and actually record the instances of the variables above. Part of the observations would be to note an exact count of instances of particular behavior as mentioned above, and part of the observation would be to provide a narrative account of the sense of play observed. In order to avoid creating anxiety of the teachers in the face of being "scrutinized" by the observers, the observers might have to be present in the role of being simply note-takers on the collaborative play experiment. Some observers would remain with the same group over successive planning sessions. Some observers would alternate between sessions either within the control groups, or within the treatment groups. Some observers would alternative between sessions and also between the control and treatment groups. In my specific case of teacher planning for example, I might ask for a center director of administrator to participant to join in under the role of a person taking notes on behalf of the rest of us.

5a. The people who will be observed/measured are...

The teacher groups will be observed, and this would include both the control and treatment groups. With the control groups, the observers will measure the same variables, determining when these things happen spontaneously, since those groups will not have any direct participants.

5b. The observing or measuring is done in the following places or situations... or derived indirectly from the following sources...

The observations will be made during the structured teacher planning meetings that have been previously established. Separate observations might be made in the form of individual interviews of the various teachers by one of the third party observers or by another administrator.

6. The observations or measurements will be analyzed in the following manner to determine whether the two situations are significantly different...

With respect to the variables above, variables 1,2, and 3 will be directly compared over several months of time to quantitatively determine whether collaborative play is successfully being introduced into the teacher planning. The final variable might depend upon a more qualitative analysis of how collaborative play seems to develop differently in control and treatment groups.

7a. Given that people who will interpret (give meaning to) the analysis are...

Those interpreting the meaning of the analysis might be school administrators and other teachers who are not participating in any collaborative planning groups.

7b. the analysis will be summarized/conveyed in the following form...

A summary will be created which indicates which of the "before","during","after" actions seem to be most closely related to the emergence of collaborative play. These will be made available to teacher and administrator groups who are developing future guidelines for planning sessions. Also, a summary of specific instances of collaborative play will be compiled as a resource for demonstrating to teachers different kinds of alternatives for ways of behaving in their planning.

—
When the results are available, the following steps can be pinned down. In the design stage, you should lay out different possibilities.

8a. The results show that what has been happening is...

Possibilities include that the "before","during", and "after" activities each show some amount of influence on the increase in collaborative play used during teacher planning. For each level of activity, it is also possible that it shows no effect on the level of collaborative play, or even is shown to be detrimental to collaborative play. Results might be inconclusive altogether because of other factors not observed in the teacher planning, such as the influence of personalities or differences in interpreting "play" by the direct participants or observers.

8b. This will be reported through the following outlets...

This will be reported in institutional annual reports, new staff orientation materials, and individual meetings between teachers and administrators.

9. What has been happening is happening because...

Will be determined by the study, but one possibility is that collaborative play is shown to be possible in teacher planning and an acceptable use of time and effort, meaning that the school as a whole might become more willing to create the environment that allows play to happen and encourage all teachers to develop the "before", "during", and "after" actions that are useful.

10. The lessons learned by sponsors of evaluation are that...

Lessons to be learned might include a deeper evaluation of why collaborative play does not happen more often, such as lack of time, feeling of apprehension, or lack of real and practical benefit. Also, the specific "before,during,after" actions might be appropriate only under certain circumstances and might need to be customized very specifically to each teacher planning group in a way that is appropriate. Future cycles of action research would likely pay great attention to the fine-tuning of the actions and even framing them in a way that allows them to evolve through the direct decision of the teachers actually carrying them out.

11. What the sponsors should now do differently is...

One possibility is that sponsors should consider how to expose the benefits of collaborative play mores teacher planning process and consider different presentations of these ideas as a way of allowing teachers to view them in ways that are most acceptable. For example, if certain teachers resist the very notion of "play" in a rigid way because they believe that it allows for silliness and makes them appear to not be serious about their work, the idea of play might be presented in alternate form, such as "experiential planning."

Development of an Action Research Project on Collaborative Play by Teachers in Curriculum Planning

Presentation Notes

<u>How Will I Describe My Progress to Others Such That Effective Feedback Can Be Given?</u>

Evaluation and Inquiry Stage:

When considering my own various experiences in adult learning, I have considered that most learning opportunities have a "feel" of work, meaning that the effort to participate fully is noticed, and there is some absence of play, experimentation, and enjoyment that might be a natural part of the process. Through my interest in collaborative play, I have wondered how I might take action to help establish a tone of collaborative play in learning opportunities and use collaborative play as a support system for allowing learning to be enjoyable.

In my background research, I have found a number of resources that describe notions such as what it means for adults to play or directions toward building collaborative learning opportunities for adults. I'm still working through these, but the ones that I have read show a general consistency in suggesting that play can be a valuable way for adults to engage with learning. One definition of play is the following: "Play: state of being that is intensely pleasurable. It energizes and enlivens us. It eases our burdens, renews a natural sense of optimism...." Many descriptions of play that I have found are similar in the way that they describe play without really defining it in a completely concrete way.

Reflection and Dialogue Epicycle:

In my own learning experiences, I have noticed that many of them have taken the form of proposing a specific goal and then indicating the path to be taken to reach that goal and then taking that path and reaching the goal. I considered that when I most enjoyed learning, there was an element of play in the situation in which I was allowed to deviate from that path and spend time on an activity which had an uncertain outcome. In a simple example, I recall a high school math teacher asking us students to try to figure out how to use a graphing calculator. There was no answer sought, just an expectation that we would discover something of use along the way. In another example, I took a continuing education class in beginning piano. The teacher interrupted the lesson to ask us to think of a song that we liked. She then asked us to try to find the correct notes to the beginning of the song on the piano keys, even when we had not yet learned note names. In both of these situations, we played. After reflecting upon this, I considered that in my ongoing adult learning settings, I might be even more rewarded if the play was collaborative – if the learners were all playing in this way but doing so in a coordinated way which we had a shared experienced that supported the development of a relationship between learners, beyond the more isolated play of the examples above. By playing, I found a very satisfied feeling from the idea that I had actually created some knowledge for myself, not simply given it directly or even prompted to find it from an external source.

Proposing and Planning Actions Stage:

After starting with a more general idea about taking action to add collaborative play to adult learning, I found new meaning during a period of much struggle and uncertainty about the purpose of my ideas. My thoughts were that play could serve as the mechanism for creating an alternative in learning to any structure that was imposed upon a group of people. In other words, play could serve as a legitimate way to support the learning itself while allowing the learners to break free from the structure that had been placed on the situation or that they had adopted for themselves. Further, I was having difficulty in defining how collaborative play could be generally placed into a situation, so I had to change my overall framework of thinking. Rather than figuring out how to build collaborative play into "any" learning opportunity as a functional action, I started to see that what I wanted to happen was for myself and other learners to simply become more sensitive to times in which play could be used to break up the structure of the learning and restore a sense of fun in learning, when appropriate. In other words, I recognized and acknowledged that I did not want to figure out how to increase the collaborative play in any situation. Instead, I realized that my hope for collaborative play was that it could be understood by learners to be an option for their style of learning at a particular time and develop the capacity to recognize this and use it. I started to understand that a slightly more narrow approach to my own action research was in order, so I renewed my focus on the specific issue of planning classroom lessons with other teachers at a preschool/afterschool center where I work. This seemed to be a natural match, since we were tasked with collaborating in order to create lesson plans and activities for students that were enjoyable for them and allowed them to play. Meanwhile, I observed that we were never really playing ourselves in the journey to accomplish this.

The general course that I took to create a plan for action took the following form.

Overview of project:
• use of collaborative play as a way to enhance learning experience for adult learners
• play = activity that has uncertain outcome which encourages experimentation, surprise, humor, and personal enjoyment
• collaborative play = play that is done by group of people in the same learning experience, such that their actions are interdependent – an act of a person during collaborative play may be a response to that of another or a prompt to further action

1. Initial thoughts
a. My interest in adult education focuses on lifelong learning and what it takes to encourage myself and other adults to develop a positive view of ongoing learning, engage in learning with a spirit of enjoyment, curiosity, and excitement, and consider how learning with others can be rewarding and create change, while at the same time taking many forms that may not be available in traditional classroom settings or educational institutions

b. First considerations – how to create an action research plan in which collaborative play is introduced into adult learning settings such that it results in an enhancement of the learning experience. Issue: could this "enhancement" be a quantifiable property?

c. Next steps – I considered what it might mean to use myself as a guinea pig in my action research. The change that I would be introducing would focus on actions that I would take, I would inquire into the way that I have been acting and how others have approached this question, and I would then evaluate the change based on my own actions and those of others.

d. Primary action research idea: - I would focus on how to develop a "Personal Engagement Plan." This would be a recipe for actions that I would take relative to three periods when encountering a learning opportunity. The idea is that prior to an upcoming well-defined learning opportunity, I would be able to create a customized Personal Engagement Plan with "before", "during", and "after" actions that I could take and then actually carry out the actions that encouraged the use of collaborative play. Evaluation would be based on determining whether or not a certain result was noticed to be different between situations that involved collaborative play, and those that didn't.

e. Emerging idea – I would focus on using my own work as a teacher to help think about how to create a Personal Engagement Plan. In my work with a youth education program, I am responsible for helping teachers develop curriculum and lesson plans for preschool and afterschool students that involve using multimedia and information literacy (primarily using computers as tools for these). The lead teachers are responsible for a level of student based on age, and this is then associated with learning goals that reflect certain subjects (reading, math, creativity, etc.). I am knowledgeable about the multimedia resources, and teachers are knowledgeable about the core topics. Neither of us understand very well each other's areas, so we must work together to create integrated activities and lesson plans for the students that account for both. Based on this need, I considered that an area for possible collaborative play was in the way that I and the other teachers could learn from each other and collaborate to plan for the activities for the students. Drawing upon the notion of collaborative play, how could I create a Personal Engagement Plan that would help to make our planning sessions more successful?

Constituency Building Epicycle:

In the development of this plan, I have been noticing that the constituency-building process has evolved somewhat naturally from the requirements of the plan itself. Primary constituents include the teachers and directors at the youth center and the students themselves. Secondary constituents include others who might observe the play that is happening in the planning sessions and those assisting me to develop the ideas for play that can be brought to the group.

A few practical areas in which this might be used realistically in the near future:
1. Preschool – upcoming planning to develop a science activity fair with the teachers to engage the kids to gain a sense of wonder and excitement about science and space
2. Afterschool – upcoming planning to develop a project that would engage the kids in creating a digital story of their personal lives

Implementation Stage:

Example of a possible Personal Engagement Plan:

To be clear, the focus is collaborative learning during the lesson planning process with teachers, not during the actually carrying out of the lesson plans with students. The following activities are those that would be done by me relative to these planning sessions.

"Before" activities:
1. observe students at play in a classroom during a more unstructured time and note specific instances in which play seems to lead to inquiry or insight
2. ask teachers for a list of possible topics that will be addressed in their classes within the following weeks
3. build a simplified prototype of a game or fun activity that might be used during a student lesson
4. find one joke, humor article, comic strip, or interesting image that is directly relevant to topics at hand or teaching
5. find a "toy" that might be relevant or interesting to the teachers

"During" activities:
1. present the joke/comic/etc. to the group
2. briefly offer the "toy" (#5 above) to the teacher group during planning and ask them to "test" it for use with the students
3. mention to the other teachers that I intend to approach our planning from a playful point of view, meaning that I would like to play with any idea before judging its value or making a decision based on it
4. make a suggestion to teachers that we play with the prototype game "as if" we were the students, and then do so if possible
5. write down suggestions made by the teachers on how to improve or clarify the game
6. ask teachers (and myself) to reflect upon the personalities of individual students and tell a story about times when they seem to be having fun
7. brainstorm ideas for an alternative game that might be developed

"After" activities:
1. make suggested changes to the prototype game
2. create additional prototype games as suggested, as possible, and present these in future planning sessions
3. make an entry in a reflective journal that describes particular moments of play between me and the other teachers

Evaluation and Inquiry Stage:

As a matter of practical evaluation of the plan, I start with a type of checklist of outcomes. The questions below highlight issues that might be changed through the introduction of collaborative play, and these generally whether or not a specific change can be observed after collaborative play has been used.

Outcomes to be measured:
Evaluation could occur by answering the following questions:
1. Did the other teachers explicitly agree to engage in play or be open to the idea?
2. Did I experience a level of enjoyment beyond the norm for teacher planning sessions?
3. Did any other teachers express that they were experiencing enjoyment during the planning session?
4. How many times was laughter elicited during the planning session?
5. Did all of my planned actions in my Personal Engagement Plan actually take place? If not, what prevented it?
6. Did the teachers and I form a concrete lesson plan for a specific period of time?
7. Did the number of interactions between the teachers and I increase between the planning session and the following one?
8. Did my understanding of the teachers' original intentions for lesson topics become more clear after the planning session? Did their understandings of my resources become more clear?
9. Over time, do the other teachers take any more initiative at bringing/suggesting new ways of play into the planning sessions?

Development of an Action Research Project on Collaborative Play by Teachers in Curriculum Planning

Narrative Outline

From Personal Action to Collaborative Play: Creating a Personal Engagement Plan for Adults that Creates a Rewarding Group Learning Experience

I. Introduction: My Perspective on Adult Learning and the Value of Play
(ties into: Evaluation of my own past scenarios, Inquiry to Illuminate the Background, Reflection)

In my own experiences in adult learning, I have become particularly interested in the idea that play may be used as a tool that might enhance the learning process by opening up the possibilities of _experimentation_ in learning. I consider this to be an important part of the learning process such that it may, when used at appropriate times, remove the boundaries of "right" and "wrong." When this happens, an opportunity for learning occurs that provides space for novel or "strange" ideas to be considered; this may not happen if learning activity is purely goal-driven, since that may require that such novel ideas are ignored if they do not directly or obviously relate to the goal. Further, if play happens in a collaborative way, this means that learners may be performing the same experiments together, finding ways to enjoy the experience, and increased sharing between them. I will reflect upon learning experiences of my own in which collaborative play did happen and work effectively as well as some that lacked such play but that might have shown a benefit from having it. Also, I will describe some initial assumptions that I made at the start of the action research.

<--->

the Introduction provides motivation and rationale for wanting to engage in the project and follow through on exploring the Background

<--->

II. Background Wisdom from the Minds and Experience of Others
(ties into: Inquiry to Illuminate the Background, Dialogue)

I will summarize my review of the literature concerning the ideas of others regarding the meaning of "play" and "collaborative play" and consider how they have been defined and related to the childhood and adult worlds of interaction. Because no single idea of play claims to be the most useful or only correct one, I will present some themes that emerge from comparing a variety of perspectives on play, and note some key contrasts. Further, I will provide some example cases of the use of play in learning situations that primarily involve adults.

<--->

the Background uncovers aspects of play as more legitimate, concrete, and realistic part of adult interaction, which suggests that change is possible in my Current Situation

<--->

III. My Current Situation and the Need for Change
(ties into: Evaluation of my current situation, Dialogue, and Constituency-Building)

I will describe the target setting of my role as a curriculum developer and teacher in a preschool program, where I need to work with a group of core preschool teachers to develop lesson plans and activities that both integrate multimedia and help meet learning standards for the students (such as literacy and science awareness). The area for change focuses on this teacher planning process itself and how collaborative play might be included in the process and used more effectively as a tool to enrich our planning, with an inner-most constituency group being these teachers.

Two central issues surround the planning process. One is that I have specialized knowledge (multimedia, technology, and information resources) and the teachers have specialized knowledge (educational standards for preschoolers and more personal knowledge of the students themselves). In order for planning to become more effective, we must learn from each other's knowledge and experience so that our plans account for all of it as much as possible. Another central issue is that planning has traditionally occurred in the form of a "decisional discussion" - a general discussion that aims to simply find agreement on a decision about what activities to use in the student classes. This means that there currently is no play between the members of the teacher planning group, even though we are attempting to create learning experiences for the students that involve high levels of play. In typical teacher planning so far, we have not really tried activities ourselves or even imagined "out loud" how they might work. My action research plan will focus on what actions I may take that can introduce the possibility of collaborative play into the teacher planning. This will be a primary area of interest in my current project.

Future cycles of action research cycle might then seek to refine how the change takes place:
• Phase 2: how to do this in such a way that the collaborative play that happens actually increases the mutual cross-learning between teachers
• Phase 3: how to do this in such a way that the collaborative play, that leads to mutual learning, also leads to more playful and well-defined student lesson plans and activities
• Phase 4: ....leads to increased engagement/enjoyment of the preschool students themselves

<--->

along with having deeper understanding of my Current Situation with respect to desired outcomes and options for achieving them, knowledge of the Background helps to point toward a path of action through the development of an Action Research Plan

<--->

IV. Developing an Action Research Plan for Change: The "Personal Engagement Plan" in Defining How Personal Action Relates to Increased Collaborative Play
(ties into: Proposing and Planning {what actions}, Implementation {strategies, logistics for action})

I will describe an idea for how to plan my actions and suggest how others might do the same across an imagined larger system of teacher planning throughout a school. My main idea is that I would create a "Personal Engagement Plan" for myself. This would be a list of actions that I would plan to take before, during, and after a teacher planning session that I propose might help to introduce collaborative play into the planning process. "Before" actions might include those that might help me to individually develop a playful attitude ahead of time and prepare materials that might be used in playful planning. "During" actions might include those that directly communicate suggestions for play to other teachers during planning and those that lead to planning activities that are themselves playful in a way that matches appropriate with the current interactions of the planning session. "After" actions might be those that allow me and others to reflect on our play and collect feedback from the observers of teacher planning.

Part of the Personal Engagement Plan will certainly require me to make attempts to define actions in the first place that I think are likely to lead to collaborative play, so I will also discuss how I might think about this. The actions might draw upon my own direct teaching and learning experiences as well as perspectives related to life experiences, such as some of my recent training in theater and kind of play that happens in sports and games.

Further, because the Personal Engagement Plan starts with myself but includes many others, I will describe how my I imagine the growth of my constituents to work over time, with respect to direct participants (myself and the other teachers), indirect participants (preschool administrators and preschool students), and allies (teachers in other schools, playful people, idea-providers, Action Research class colleagues). This description will include how I might ideally frame the constituency in a holistic way, such that I am able to offer support to constituents as they do so with me, and such that communication/relationship-building might occur not only between me and individual constituents and constituent groups, but between constituents themselves. Because collaboration and play lie at the foundation of the change that I envision, constituency-building will also involve specifically seeking out skeptical people who can help me to consider objections to the use of collaborative play or areas in which play in general might be met with resistance.

<--->
reflecting on the Development of an Action Research Plan, helps to uncover a starting point of actual small- and medium-scale actions that I might employ as a first attempt of a Personal Engagement Plan
<--->

V. Example Personal Engagement Plan
(ties into: Implementation, Reflection, Constituency-Building))

Because the Personal Engagement Plan is the primary vehicle for supporting the actions taken to create change, I will provide a suggestion for an initial plan while considering how this might work in my own situation, as well as proposing how it might also apply to an imagined situation in a larger environment where multiple teacher planning sessions might be happening, where collaborative play is sought not only as a tool for in-group teacher planning but also as a new element of school/institution culture. I am now considering that My own Personal Engagement Plan might involve the integration of several elements: 1) lists of "before", "during", and "after" actions that I take, 2) conditional statements/priorities that regulate when certain actions need not or may not be taken relative to a particular teacher planning session, and 3) time-based and systems-thinking considerations that influence overall implementation of the actions, i.e., does implementing a given action disrupt some other part of the system of the preschool that otherwise appears to exist outside of teacher planning sessions?

<--->
the perspective of a concrete Personal Engagement Plan suggests how change may be measured through the specific guidelines of an explicit Evaluation
<--->

VI. Evaluation of the Personal Engagement Plan
(ties into: Evaluation, Dialogue, Constituency-Building)

Consideration of the Personal Engagement Plan will also include description of how this can be evaluated. Because collaborative play might not be equally meaningful or perfectly well-defined across all teachers, evaluation will depend not only upon my own reflection but also on feedback/commentary given directly by other teachers, notes on observations made by third-party observers, and other quantitative and qualitative measurements of my own and others' behavior both during and outside of the teacher planning sessions.

<--->
the results of the Evaluation will may help to refine the Personal Engagement Plan not only in terms of specific actions but also in terms of how all of the specific actions work together, and revised actions may then propel the action research toward Future Cycles
<--->

VII. Imagining Further Iterations of the Action Research Cycles
(ties into: Evaluation, Inquiry {unanswered questions related to Personal Engagement Plan})

The primary focus of the action research during the first phase will be to introduce collaborative play into the teacher planning process in some form, as a way of discovering which actions that I take might catalyze the collaborative play interactions that take place. This not only means injecting "instances" of collaborative play into the formal teacher planning sessions, but also hopefully taking the actions that help to establish that the overall environment allows for collaborative play where it might even become more spontaneous outside of the formal planning. Future directions of the action research might then address the types of implied changes that are suggested under Phase 2, 3, 4, and beyond, as mentioned previously under the "Current Situation" section.

4
CONNECTIONS & EXTENSIONS

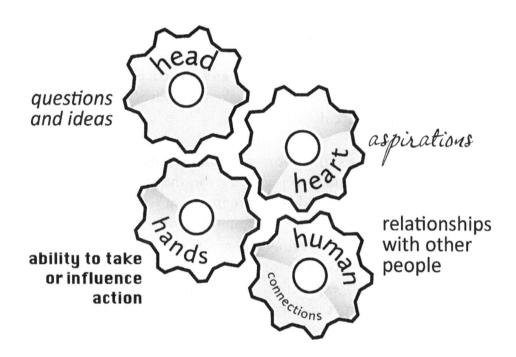

questions
and ideas

aspirations

ability to take
or influence
action

relationships
with other
people

TEACHING and LEARNING for REFLECTIVE PRACTICE

Taking Yourself Seriously is designed for anyone who wants to integrate "head, heart, hands, and human connections" in their research and writing. The intended audience is not limited to students. Nevertheless, a pedagogical current is obvious—the book's origins lie in Peter's research and writing courses; the **Phases** and **Cycles and Epicycles** frameworks are designed to be translated readily into assignments, classes, and stages of semester-long student projects; and theses or dissertations fit well under the category of a **Synthesis of Theory and Practice**. The pedagogical challenges of teaching students to take themselves seriously warrant, therefore, some more discussion.

What follows takes the form of *snapshots* from Peter's journey teaching research and other courses for the Critical and Creative Thinking (CCT) Graduate Program at the University of Massachusetts Boston. CCT, despite the "thinking" in its name, is about changing and reflecting on *practice*. The Program aims to provide its mid-career or career-changing students with "knowledge, tools, experience, and support so they can become constructive, reflective agents of change in education, work, social movements, science, and creative arts" (CCT 2008). In this vein, it seems less important for us to describe the detail of the classroom mechanics and CCT course requirements, than to stimulate reflection and dialogue about the challenge of supporting students (and others) to develop as reflective practitioners.

A book cannot recreate for readers the experience of participating in classroom activities and the unfolding process of a program of studies. Even so, some readers might want us to explicate our line of thinking and relate it to what others have written and done. We do not, however, attempt that. Instead, we offer the snapshots in a spirit of opening up questions and pointing to a complexity of relevant considerations, not of pinning down answers with tight evidence. We encourage readers to participate in the online forum that accompanies this book (see Resources section later in Part 4) so as to engage the authors and each other in ongoing conversation and in sharing resources, struggles, and accomplishments.

* * *

1. Goals of research and engagement; goals of developing as a reflective practitioner

Each of the **Phases of Research and Engagement** is defined by a goal. I (Peter) made the phases and goals explicit after my first semester teaching research and writing to CCT's mid-career graduate students. One student, an experienced teacher, had dutifully submitted assignments, such as the **Annotated Bibliography**, all the time expressing skepticism that this course was teaching her anything new: "I have already taken research courses and know how to do research papers." Indeed, I felt that most of her submissions did not help move her project forward; the form was there, but not the substance. I often asked her to revise and resubmit, emphasizing that the point was not to complete, say, the annotated bibliography just because I, the instructor, deemed this an essential part of a research project. The point was for her to do the annotated bibliography in a way that brought her closer to being able to say "I know what others have done before, either in the form of writing or action, that informs and connects with my project, and I know what others are doing now." By the end of the semester I had made such goals and the corresponding **Phases** an explicit organizing structure for the course and other research projects. The resistance of this student had given me an invaluable push to rework my own syllabus.

The goals of research and engagement represented, however, only half of what was going on in the research and writing course. I identified ten additional goals related to the process of pursuing a major research and writing project. Over the next year, helped by some teacher research (snapshot 2), I refined these **Reflective Practitioner Goals**. I have since incorporated both sets of goals into a **Self-Assessment** that students complete at the end of the research and writing course as well as at the end of their studies. (See also **Assessment that Keeps the Attention Away from Grades** in a way that is consistent with the two sets of goals, required **Personal and Professional Development Workbook**, and other expectations for **Research Organization**.)

2. Making space for taking initiative in and through relationships

I want students to see **Dialogue around Written Work** as an important part of defining and refining research direction and questions. However, students are familiar with the system of submit a product, receive a grade, check that assignment off the to-do list, then move on to the next one. They know that they have to expose their submissions to the instructor, but are uncomfortable about subjecting their work to dialogue. My challenge, then, has been to get students into the swing of an unfamiliar system as quickly as possible so they can begin to experience its benefits.

I chose to focus on this challenge when I participated in a faculty seminar on "Becoming a teacher-researcher" during my second year teaching CCT students (Taylor 1999). A month into semester the students in the research and writing course completed a survey about their expectations and concerns in working under what they called the "revise and resubmit" process. The participants in the faculty seminar then reviewed all the students' responses and brainstormed about qualities of an improved system and experience. We wrote suggestions on large Post-its, which we grouped and gave names to. Five categories or themes emerged: "negotiate power/standards," "horizontal community," "develop autonomy," "acknowledge affect," and "be here now."

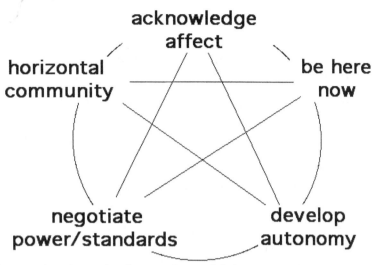

Five themes about improving the experience of dialogue around written work. (A sixth theme, "explore difference," was added later.)

In the following class I initiated discussion with the students around their responses and the themes generated by the faculty seminar. We clarified the meaning of the themes and explored the tensions between them (conveyed by the connecting lines in the figure above). For example, "develop autonomy" stood for digesting comments and making something for oneself—neither treating comments as dictates nor insulating oneself by keeping from the eyes of others. Yet, "negotiate power/standards" recognized that students made assumptions about my ultimate power over grades, which translated into their thinking that I expected them to take up my suggestions. These assumptions about the "vertical" relationship between instructor and student do have to be aired and addressed, but "horizontal community" captured the need for students to put effort into building other kinds of relationship.

During the rest of the semester, class discussions continued to refer to the themes and tensions. We applied them to the whole research and engagement process, not only to dialogue around written work. I looked for a substitute for "autonomy" after some students construed this word as going their own way and not responding to comments of others, including their instructors. When "taking initiative" was suggested by my wife, I realized that it applied to all five themes. I emailed my students: "[The challenge is to] take initiative in building horizontal relationships, in negotiating power/standards, in acknowledging that affect is involved in what you're doing and not doing (and in how others respond to that), in clearing away distractions from other sources (present and past) so you can be here now." Don't wait for the instructor to tell you how to solve an expository problem, what must be read and covered in a literature review, or what was meant by some comment you don't understand. Don't put off giving your writing to the instructor or to other readers and avoid talking to them because you're worried that they don't see things the same way as you do.

A longer phrase soon emerged: "Taking initiative in *and through* relationships." That is, don't expect to learn or change on one's own. Build relationships with others; interact with them. This doesn't mean bowing down to their views, but take them in and work them into your own reflective inquiry until you can convey more powerfully to them what you are about (which may or may not have changed as a result of the reflective inquiry). Finally, do not expect learning or change to happen without jostling among the five themes-in-tension. The themes do not always pull you in the same direction, so your focus might move from one to another, rather than trying to attend to all of them simultaneously.

Of course, laying out this "mandala" did not specify *how* to teach and support students to take progressively more initiative. Nevertheless, I believe that talking about the five points helped the students recognize themselves and take more initiative in their learning relationships. Since then I have presented the insights from the original group to new cohorts—often adding "explore difference" as a sixth theme.

(Presenting an analysis or action plan developed by a previous group is never as powerful as a group creating its own. Given this,

I have asked each new cohort in the research and writing course to contribute to ongoing teacher research around the question: "By what means can the group function as a support and coaching structure to get most students to finish their reports by the end of the semester?"; see **Support and Coaching Structure**).

3. Opening wide and focusing in

A colleague in the faculty seminar on teacher research (snapshot 2) participated in the first class of the research and writing course as if he were a student. The class consisted of: an overview of the phases from me; a Q&A session with a student from the previous year's class (during which I was absent from the room); and some freewriting, rough drafting, and peer sharing of an initial project description. The colleague, Emmett Schaeffer, commented afterwards on the oscillation the students faced between opening wide and focusing in. He also noted that the students were somewhat "dazed" about how much was opened up and put in play during this first session (Box 1). As my thank you email expressed (Box 2), having someone else see what was going on helped me articulate and own a tension that runs through most of my teaching.

Box 1. Comments from a colleague on the student experience at the start of the research and writing course

→ on "divergent" thinking
certainly, at first, and, if I understand correctly, throughout the process,
you think one engaged in research and engagement should remain open, both to others and their opinions, but also to one's "divergent" (from one's conscious, explicitly formulated path) thinking, feeling, etc.
--sort of [1] opening wide, [2] focusing and formulating,

[1] the "opening wide" could take the form of:

any less than fully formulated thinking
free writing
sharing (with a partner, teacher, group) one's formulations
(written or oral)

then,

being fully attentive to what one has expressed (intended or
otherwise), as well as to feedback

[2] the focusing and formulating stage could take the form of:

oral/written formulations with an explicit purpose and more
(always simply comparative) fully formulated

→ what about students being "dazed," "overwhelmed" and "confused"?
(and perhaps not only at the beginning)
My guess as to purpose:
(of course partly you don't choose this outcome, it's rather a function
of students' previous training but to some extent I think it's inherent
in your approach and philosophy)

1. experiential learning – It'll become clear through doing it
(and reflecting on the doing that requires some doing).
2. everything up in the air (not settled, in place, foreclosed, etc.)
to maximize
   a. vision of possible outcomes
   b. their agency in influencing settling
   c. model of anxiety and confusion inherent (at first) in
   sharing and remaining open, while proceeding to try various
   ways to "sort things out"

Box 2. Thank you email about the affirmation-articulation connection

Emmett,
I really appreciate your keen observations and the work you did in
synthesizing them into the notes. What we did together was rare
and special -- I could only remember one other time I got a
colleague's observations that affirmed but also helped me articulate
and own what I was doing. That time was an ESL and Spanish
teacher who had asked to visit a class of mine about biology and
society. She noted my comfortable use of ambiguity. Much followed

for me from her naming this. In fact, I suspect that the affirmation-articulation connection is a key to the observed person doing something productive with the observations.
Thanks,
Peter

4. From educational evaluation to constituency building

The same observation about having to move between opening out and focusing in was made independently a few years later by a student, herself an experienced college teacher, when she summarized the experience of the course on evaluation and action research. Snapshots 1 to 3 have not mentioned that course, but it was evolving at the same time as the course on research and writing. When I first took over teaching this second course, the title and emphasis was educational evaluation. I soon had this changed to evaluation of educational change so as to clarify that it was not about assessment of students. Moreover, to meet the needs of the diverse, mid-career professionals and creative artists that enter CCT, "educational change" had to be construed broadly to include organizational change, training, and personal development, as well as curricular and school change.

The revised title still missed the central motivation for the course in the CCT curriculum, which was: "If you have good ideas, how do you get others to adopt or adapt them?" Put in other words: "How do you build a constituency around your idea?" This concern can lead researchers into evaluating how good the ideas actually are (with respect to some defined objectives) so they can demonstrate this to others. It can also lead a researcher to work with others to develop the idea so it becomes theirs as well and thus something they are invested in.

Taking an individual who wants "to do something to change the current situation, that is, to take action" as the starting point, Action Research became the central thread. The course title was eventually changed again to reflect the emphasis on Action Research for Educational, Professional and Personal Change. The "**Cycles and Epicycles**" model that emerged made room for group facilitation, participatory planning, and reflective practice, as well as for systematic evaluation. The next two snapshots touch on group processes; the one after links the research side of Action Research to Problem-Based Learning.

5. Conditions for a successful workshop

My own research during the 1980s and 1990s focused on the complexity of ecological or environmental situations and of the social situations in which the environmental research is undertaken. Since the 1990s collaboration has become a dominant concern in environmental planning and management, although the need to organize collaborative environmental research can be traced back at least into the 1960s (Taylor et al. 2008). Collaboration is self-consciously organized through the frequent use of workshops and other "organized multi-person collaborative processes" (OMPCPs).

I started to try to make more sense of the workshop form after participating during the first half of 2000 in four innovative, interdisciplinary workshops primarily in the environmental arena (Taylor 2001). Two ideals against which I assessed these workshops were that group processes can: a) result in collaborators' investment in the product of the processes; and b) ensure that knowledge generated is greater than any single collaborator or sum of collaborators came in with (see discussion in Part 4 of strategic participatory planning). As a postscript to my analysis of why a workshop (or OMPCP) might be needed to address the complexity of environmental issues, I assembled a list of guidelines or heuristics about making workshops in general work.

At my first presentation on this topic there was in the audience a professional facilitator, Tom Flanagan, who offered to help me develop a more systematic set of principles for bringing about successful workshops. The process he led me through involved:

- a. Defining my criteria for a *successful* workshop;
- b. Rephrasing the heuristics as conditions that might contribute directly or indirectly to these criteria being fulfilled;
- c. Answering a set of questions of the form: "Would addressing condition A significantly help in achieving condition B?"

The results of steps a and b are given in Box 3. The questions in step c were generated by CogniSystem software that analyzed my responses and then arranged the conditions in a "structural model" from "deep" to "top," where deeper conditions are helpful for the ones above them.

Box 3. Criteria and Conditions for a Successful Workshop

A. Two criteria of success
i) the outcome is larger and more durable than what any one participant came in with. Durable means
- a) the participants are engaged in carrying out or carrying on the knowledge and plans they develop; and
- b) the knowledge is applied and has significance.
ii) participants' subsequent work enhances the capacity of others to flexibly engage, that is, to connect with people who are able to take initiative—or are almost able to—in forming communities of practice/change collaborations that provide their participants experiences that enhance their ability to flexibly engage.

B. Conditions that might contribute directly or indirectly to these criteria being fulfilled
- it brings to the surface knowledge of the participants that they were not able, at first, to acknowledge.
- participants get to know more about each others' not-yet-stable aspects.
- quiet spaces that occur are not filled up.
- participants recognize that there is insight in every response.
- the facilitator invites participants to share the experience of being unsure, but excitable.
- the facilitator provides participants with the image of a workshop as a journey into unknown areas or allowing them to see familiar areas in a fresh light. (A workshop/journey involves risk; requires support; creates more experiences than can be integrated at first sight; yields personal changes.)
- participants gain insight into their present place and direction by hearing what they happen to mention and omit in telling their own stories.
- participants are heard.
- participants hear others and hear themselves better as a result of being

heard.
- this hearing of others leads participants to examine decisions made in advance about what the other people are like, what they are and are not capable of.
- participants inquire further on the issues that arise in their own projects.
- participants inquire further into how they support the work of others.
- participants' energies are mobilized by the process.
- there is a wide range of participants, not only technically expert participants.
- the plans allow for individual participants to select and focus on a subset of the workshop-generated specific plans or knowledge in their subsequent work.
- the process, as a learning community, enables participants to ask for help and support during the workshop.
- the process, as a learning community, enables participants to develop relationships that will enable them keep getting help and support when the workshop is over.
- participants find opportunities to affirm what is working well.
- the reflection on each phase leads to one concrete product to take into next phase.
- the experiences of the workshop enhance the ability of the participants to flexibly engage.

Tom's intention was only to introduce me to structural modeling, not to lead me systematically through the full process, so I should not over-interpret the outcome of our computer-aided analysis. I include here only the deepest three layers and the top of the model to help readers picture a structural model (see figure below). Let me draw attention, however, to the deepest condition, "quiet spaces that occur are not filled up." It is no small challenge for someone organizing or facilitating a workshop (or OMPCP) to ensure that this condition is met. Conversely, when we try to squeeze too much in a limited time and the quiet spaces condition is not met, we should not be surprised that the criteria for a successful workshop are not achieved.

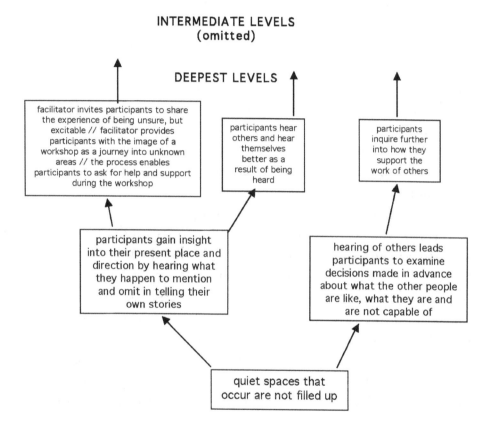

TOP LEVEL

the process, as a learning community, enables participants to develop relationships that will enable them keep getting help and support when the workshop is over

the experiences of the workshop enhance the ability of the participants to flexibly engage

INTERMEDIATE LEVELS
(omitted)

DEEPEST LEVELS

facilitator invites participants to share the experience of being unsure, but excitable // facilitator provides participants with the image of a workshop as a journey into unknown areas // the process enables participants to ask for help and support during the workshop

participants hear others and hear themselves better as a result of being heard

participants inquire further into how they support the work of others

participants gain insight into their present place and direction by hearing what they happen to mention and omit in telling their own stories

hearing of others leads participants to examine decisions made in advance about what the other people are like, what they are and are not capable of

quiet spaces that occur are not filled up

Extracts from the structural model

6. Four R's of developing as a collaborator

Group processes not only need skillful and effective facilitators; they also need participants or collaborators who are skilled and effective in contributing to the desired outcomes. To develop skills and dispositions of collaboration requires researchers (and researchers-in-training) to make opportunities for practicing what they have been introduced to and to persist even when they encounter resistance. What moves them to pursue such development?

I have had an opportunity since 2004 to address this issue through an annual series of experimental, interaction-intensive, interdisciplinary workshops "to foster collaboration among those who teach, study, and engage with the public about scientific developments and social change." The workshops are documented in detail on their websites (NewSSC 2008), but a thumbnail sketch would be: They are small, with international, interdisciplinary participants of mixed rank (i.e., from graduate students to professors). There is no delivery of papers. Instead participants lead each other in activities, designed before or developed during the workshops, that can be adapted to college classrooms and other contexts. They also participate in group processes that are regular features of the workshops and are offered as models or tools to be adapted or adopted in other contexts. The themes vary from year to year, but each workshop lasts four days and moves through four broad, overlapping phases: exposing diverse points of potential interaction; focusing on detailed case study; activities to engage participants in each others' projects; and taking stock. The informal and guided opportunities to reflect on hopes and experiences during the workshop produce feedback that shapes the unfolding program as well as changes in the design of subsequent workshops.

The ongoing evolution of the workshops has been stimulated not only by written and spoken evaluations, but also by an extended debriefing immediately following each workshop and by advisory group discussions, such as one in 2008 that addressed the question of what moves people develop themselves as collaborators. A conjecture emerged that this development happens when participants see an experience or training as transformative. After reviewing the evaluations we identified four "R's"—respect, risk, revelation, and re-engagement—as conditions that make interactions among participants transformative (Box 4; see Taylor et al. 2011 for elaboration and supporting quotations from the evaluations). A larger set of R's for personal and professional development will be presented in snapshot 9 (indeed, the larger set pre-dated and influenced the formulation of these 4R's).

Box 4. Four R's that make interactions among researchers transformative

1. Respect. The small number and mixed composition of the workshop participants means that participants have repeated exchanges with those who differ from them. Many group processes promote listening to others and provide the experience of being listened to. Participation in the activities emphasizes that each participant, regardless of background or previous experience has something valuable to contribute to the process and outcomes. In these and other ways, respect is not simply stated as a ground rule, but is enacted.

2. Risk. Respect creates a space with enough safety for participants to take risks of various kinds, such as, speaking personally during the autobiographical introductions, taking an interest in points of view distant in terms of discipline and experience, participating—sometimes quite playfully—during unfamiliar processes, and staying with the process as the workshop unfolds or "self-organizes" without an explicit agreement on where it is headed and without certainty about how to achieve desired outcomes.

3. Revelation. A space is created by respect and risk in which participants bring to the surface thoughts and feelings that articulate, clarify and complicate their ideas, relationships, and aspirations—in short, their identities. In the words of one participant: "The various activities do not simply build connections with others, but they necessitate the discovery of the identity of others through their own self-articulations. But since those articulations follow their own path, one sees them not as simple reports of some static truth but as new explorations of self, in each case. Then one discovers this has happened to oneself as much as to others-one discovers oneself anew in the surprising revelations that emerge in the process of self-revelation."

4. Re-engagement. Respect, risk, and revelation combine so that participants' "gears" engage. This allows them to sustain quite a high level of energy during throughout the workshop and engage actively with others. Equally important, participants are reminded of their aspirations to work in supportive communities—thus, the prefix *re*-engage. Participants say they discover new possibilities for working with others on ideas related to the workshop topic.

7. Problem-based learning

In contrast to the step-by-step progression in most accounts of action research, the "cycles and epicycles" model allows for extensive reflection and dialogue. This is essential not only for constituency-building, but also for problem-finding, that is, for ongoing rethinking of the nature of the situation and the actions appropriate to improving it. In this sense action research mirrors Problem-Based Learning (PBL), at least the kind of PBL that begins from a scenario in which the problems are not well defined (Greenwald 2000). Stimulated by the work of my CCT colleague, Nina Greenwald, I began to introduce a PBL approach in the evaluation course which led it evolve into an Action Research course. I then brought PBL into other courses on science in its social context. The way I have come to teach with PBL is given in Box 5 (extracted from Taylor 2008a, which includes links to examples of PBL scenarios and student work).

Box 5. Problem-Based Learning, an Overview

Students brainstorm so as to identify a range of problems related to an instructor-supplied scenario then choose which of these they want to investigate and report back on. The problem definitions may evolve as students investigate and exchange findings with peers. If the scenario is written well, most of the problems defined and investigated by the students will relate to the subject being taught, but instructors have to accept some "curve balls" in return for
- student engagement in self-invented inquiry;
- content coverage by the class as a whole; and
- increased motivation for subsequent, more-focused inquiry (see "inverted pedagogy" below).

Four features of this PBL are worth noting:

Interdisciplinary Coaching: The instructors facilitate the brainstorming and student-to-student exchange and support, coach the students in their individual tasks, and serve as resource persons by providing contacts and reading suggestions drawn from their longstanding interdisciplinary work and experience.

Inverted pedagogy: The experience of PBL is expected to motivate students to identify and pursue the disciplinary learning and disciplined inquiry they need to achieve the competencies and impact they desire. (This inverts the conventional curriculum in which command of fundamentals is a prerequisite for application of our learning to real cases.)

KAQF framework for inquiry and exchange: This asks students to organize their thinking and research with an eye on what someone might do, propose, or plan on the basis of the results, presumably actions that address the objective stated in the PBL scenario.

Internet facilitation: The internet makes it easier to explore strands of inquiry beyond any well-packaged sequence of canonical readings, to make rapid connections with experts and other informants, and to develop evolving archives of materials and resources that can be built on by future classes and others.

PBL was enthusiastically pursued by one CCT student and led to her transformation from community-college librarian with no science background to participant in campaigns around health disparities and employment as a research assistant in the biomedical area. Although I will not tell her story here, it moves me to recount some earlier reflections on students' development in the CCT Program as a whole, which make up the last two snapshots.

8. Journeying

One course I taught for the first time after I joined the CCT Program was "Critical Thinking." Mid-way through the first semester, when the topic was revising lesson plans, we revisited a demonstration I had made during the first class. The details are not important here, except to say that some students had interpreted the demonstration as a science lesson even though the science aspect seemed unimportant to me. Discussion of the discrepancy led me to articulate my primary goal more clearly, which was that students would puzzle over the general conundrum of how questions that retrospectively seem obvious ever occur to us. That puzzle was meant to lead into considering how we might be susceptible to further re-seeings. The image that arose for me during the discussion was that a person's development as a critical thinker is like undertaking a personal journey into unfamiliar or unknown areas. Both involve risk, open up questions, create more experiences than can be integrated at first sight, require support, yield personal change, and so on. This journeying metaphor differs markedly from the conventional philosophical view of critical thinking as scrutinizing the reasoning, assumptions, and evidence behind claims (Ennis 1987, Critical Thinking Across The Curriculum Project 1996). Instead of the usual connotations of "critical" with judgement and finding fault according to some standards (Williams 1983, 84ff), journeying draws attention to the inter- and intra-personal dimensions of people developing their thinking and practice.

The image of critical thinking as journeying gave me a hook to make sense of my development as a teacher. In narrating my own journey, I attempted to expose my own conceptual and practical struggles in learning how to decenter pedagogy without denying the role I had in providing space and support for students' development as critical thinkers (Taylor 2008b, but written circa 2000). The central challenge I identified was that of helping people make knowledge and practice from insights and experience that they are not prepared, at first, to acknowledge—something that seems relevant to teaching research and engagement as well as critical thinking. Several related challenges for the teacher or facilitator emerged, which are summarized in Box 6.

Box 6. Helping people make knowledge and practice from insights and experience that they are not prepared, at first, to acknowledge

Teacher-facilitators should:
a) Help students to generate questions about issues they were not aware they faced.
b) Acknowledge and mobilize the diversity inherent in any group, including the diversity of mental, emotional, situational, and relational factors that people identify as making re-seeing possible.
c) Help students clear mental space so that thoughts about an issue in question can emerge that had been below the surface of their attention.
d) Teach students to listen well. (Listening well seemed to help students tease out alternative views. Without alternatives in mind scrutiny of one's own evidence, assumptions and logic, or of those of others is difficult to motivate or carry out; see also point i, below. Being listened to, in turn,

seems to help students access their intelligence—to bring to the surface, reevaluate, and articulate things they already know in some sense.)

e) Support students on their journeys into unfamiliar or unknown areas (see paragraph above).

f) Encourage students to take initiative in and through relationships (see snapshots 2 and 3 above).

g) Address fear felt by students and by oneself as their teacher.

h) Have confidence and patience that students will become more invested in the process and the outcomes when insights emerge from themselves.

i) Raise alternatives. (Critical thinking depends on inquiry being informed by a strong sense of how things could be otherwise. People understand things better when they have placed established facts, theories, and practices in tension with alternatives.)

j) Introduce and motivate "opening up themes," that is, propositions that are simple to convey, but always point to the greater complexity of particular cases and to further work needed to study those cases (Taylor 2005).

k) Be patient and persistent about students taking up the alternatives, themes, and other tools and applying them to open up questions in new areas. (Experiment and experience are needed for students—and for teachers—to build up a set of tools that work for them.)

l) Take seriously the creativity and capacity-building that seems to follow from well-facilitated participation (see snapshots 5 and 6), while still allowing space for researchers to insert the "trans-local," that is, their analysis of changes that arise beyond the local region and span a larger scale than the local.

9. Many R's

When the CCT graduate program was moved under a Department of Curriculum and Instruction, I decided to learn more about the theory that guided that field. I came across Doll's (1993) account of postmodern curriculum design, which centers on his "4R's": richness, recursion, relation, and rigor. My immediate response was that Doll's R's do not capture a lot of what goes into CCT students' mid-career personal and professional development. I soon had twelve R's, and then more. The figure below took shape as I played with ways to convey that some R's will make limited sense until more basic Rs have been internalised and that opening-out periods alternate with periods of consolidating experiences to date.

journeying inquirer

focusing in — *opening out*

Reading

Review

Reasoning w/ respect to evidence & alternatives

Relationship w/ oneself (moving towards autonomy)

Reflection & metacognition

wRiting

Relationships w/ peers & allies (dialogue & collaboration)

Risk & experiment

Rest

Rearrange, adapt & create

Reception: being Read, heard, & Reviewed

Relationships w/ authority (negotiate power & standards)

Revision (incl. dialogue around written work)

Relaxation

Research & evaluation (learning from the work of others & your own)

Respect (explore difference)

Responsibility (concern w/ aims, means & consequences)

Repose

Recursion & practice (address same concern from many angles & in variety of settings)

Reevaluation (of emotions at root of responses) so as to better take initiative

Reconstruction (personal/organizational/social change)

reflective practitioner
wholehearted, responsible engagement with others
"Head, Heart, Hands & Human Connection"

The Rs of personal and professional development

I sometimes present this schema to students as a way to take stock of their own development. I suggest that they reflect at the end of each semester. For as many Rs as make sense, they should give an example and articulate their current sense of the meaning of any given R. I also use the many R's to remind myself as a teacher to expect the flow of any student's development to be windy and less than direct. (In this sense the schema of many R's stands as a counterpoint to the popular idea of backward design in curriculum, that is: identify desired results; determine acceptable evidence of students achieving those results; plan learning experiences and instruction accordingly, making explicit the sought-after results and evidence; Wiggins and McTighe 2005.)

* * *

The snapshots from Peter's journey suggest a windy and less-than-direct flow of development as a teacher and facilitator of research and engagement. Although we can imagine readers thinking they need to see more of the action and background behind the snapshots, we will not try to fill in more. Instead, we end with the hope that the account of this pedagogical journey, together with the tools and frameworks of Parts 1 and 2 as well as the illustrations in Part 3, help you move ahead in your own journeys of research and engagement—journeys in which you take risks, open up questions, create more experiences than can be integrated at first sight, require support, and generate personal and professional change.

ACTION RESEARCH and PARTICIPATION

Action Research has been given many meanings (Greenwood and Levin 1998, Kemmis and McTaggart 2005). In this section we position our **Cycles and Epicycles for Action Research** framework (Part 1) in relation to three sources of inspiration for us: Participatory Action Research; Strategic Participatory Planning of the Institute of Cultural Affairs; and the Highlander Center.

> We did make a terrible lot of mistakes... So we had a little self-criticism, and we said, what we know, the solutions we have, are for the problems that people don't have. And we're trying to solve their problems by saying they have the problems that we have the solutions for. That's academia, so it won't work...
>
> So what we've got to do is to unlearn much of what we've learned, and then try to learn how to learn from the people. Myles Horton (in Horton and Moyers 1983)

In the introduction to the Action Research we posit an individual, such as a student, wanting "to do something to change the current situation, that is, to take action," and then building a constituency for that action. "Constituency building happens in a number of ways: when you draw people into reflection, dialogue, and other participatory processes in order to elicit ideas about the current situation, clarify objectives, and generate ideas and plans about taking action to improve the situation; when people work together to implement actions; and when people see evaluations of how good the actions or changes were in achieving the objectives." Some texts on Action Research emphasize the last aspect—evaluation (or data collection and analysis)—as if research (or evidence) is key to achieving change. But there are too many research reports gathering dust and too many researchers lamenting that the results of their research have been ignored by policy-makers and leaders. To avoid that, assuming you take your ideas for change seriously enough to want others to adopt or adapt them, you can emphasize constituency building throughout the Action Research cycle and epicycles.

This book's emphasis on constituency building is informed and inspired by Participatory Action Research (PAR), in which social scientists shape their inquiries through on-going work with and empowerment of the people most affected by some aspect of economic or social change. Greenwood and Levin (1998, 173-185) review various approaches to PAR (see also Park et al. 1993; Selener 1993; Denzin and Lincoln 2005), but the power of participation is better conveyed by accounts of the struggles of local peoples to influence science and politics, e.g., Adams (1975); Gibbs (1982); Brown (2007). PAR or its cognates are widely promoted in rural development in poor areas of the world, from which cases are often drawn to illustrate the rise of citizen participation and of new institutions of civil society (Burbidge 1997). The following example of PAR in agroforestry is drawn from Taylor (2005, 204ff).

Whose trees are these?
In the mid-1980s CARE, an international aid and development organization, decided to respond to the excessive removal of trees in agricultural areas in western Kenya. They embarked on a project to establish an extension system that would promote and provide support for tree planting by farmers on their holdings. CARE sought to overcome the shortcomings of previous agroforestry projects in the Sahelian region of Africa, which had largely failed—one estimate of the average cost those projects had incurred for each surviving tree was $500. At the same time, CARE wanted a research component built in to analyze systems of farm production, not only of crops, but also of things necessary to basic household needs, such as for energy, shelter, and water. The research aimed to tease out the trade-offs, constraints and benefits in growing trees within those systems (Vonk 1987).

The leaders of this development project, agroforesters Remko Vonk and Louise Buck, identified that one reason for previous failures was that the community-based nurseries and plantations of previous projects had left the beneficiaries of the tree products and timber ill-defined (Vonk 1987).

Many of the local participants saw the tree planting as someone else's project, and thought the benefits would not likely come their way. Vonk and Buck reasoned that if trees were planted on individual farms, the ownership would be clearer; the local Kenyans implementing the project would also be the ones reaping the benefits. Moreover, the project leaders aimed to facilitate local participation in the design and evaluation stages of the project. In pursuing this, they drew upon their experience in a pilot project and upon the experience of others in previous health care extension projects.

This combination of local and outside influence characterized the project as it developed. First, CARE only entered only the farming communities that invited them. Initial interviews were conducted to learn about the existing use of trees on and off the farms: Which trees are being used; which had been used; which could be used? What are the reasons for not planting trees? Much of the interviewing was conducted by extension workers who CARE directors trained not to transmit information, but instead to "Respect, Encourage, Ask, and Listen." In response to information emerging from the interviews, CARE's preliminary plan of planting four species was modified to allow for selections from a menu of forty-eight species. The techniques of cultivation that the researchers adopted, using indigenous systems as a starting point, were understandable to the farmers and could be managed by them within their labor and other seasonal constraints. In turn, the extension agents' connection with farmers helped them plan, monitor, collect data on, and analyze the different tree-planting arrangements.

The resulting agroforestry practices and results differed markedly from those of previous systems and from the approaches of CARE's agroforestry specialists, which had been on trees that would directly serve agriculture, for example, by fixing nitrogen and making it available in the soil. The case of *Markhamia platyclayx* is illustrative. This species, virtually unmentioned in the agroforestry literature, was the most commonly found species in cropland in the district. The tree did not enhance crop growth, but, as interviews with the farmers revealed, *M. platyclayx* grew quickly and so was used to demarcate family compounds and plots. Reduction in crop production because of shading and root competition could be minimized if the trees were pruned regularly. The leaves became a source of mulch and compost, and scattered trees contributed to soil conservation and had a windbreak effect that protected the crops in the fields. The trees could be cut for poles when cash income was needed. They could be used to provide timber or shade. Finally, the leaves were used in preparing food and in medicines. CARE research confirmed that farmers generally knew how to manage the species well for these different uses. At the same time, CARE was able to help the farmers by contributing research results on the optimal time for harvesting of trees to be used for poles and on possible causes of seedling death.

In general, the trees that farmers favored turned out to have the following characteristics: They tended to require low management. They were inter-cropped with crops or even interspersed throughout the fields; they were not only planted as hedgerows. Their products, such as firewood and poles for building, sometimes compensated for the negative impact they had on the yields of adjacent crops. Over and above these characteristics, other factors influencing use of different tree species on particular farms or more generally included: the history of different farms, in particular, where family compounds had been abandoned leaving its trace in nutrients from feces and ashes, and how land had been subdivided among sons; the different needs of men and women; and the need for firewood in areas close to Lake Victoria in order to smoke or fry Nile perch (a species that, unlike the fish it has displaced since being introduced to the Lake in the 1950s, is too oily to be sun-dried).

CARE's project involved researchers' collaboration not only with farmers, but also with community groups. For example, researchers worked with schools to establish seedling nurseries. When termite removal of seeds became a problem, the project leaders insisted that pesticides not be used near schoolchildren and sought non-toxic solutions. Some control schemes suggested by the community members failed, but success was eventually achieved following some farmers' recommendation that seeds be surrounded with ashes. Again, in the spirit of collaboration, one CARE official's innovation of using plastic to avoid dampening the ashes when watering the crops reduced the number of times the ashes had to be reapplied.

This combination of local and outside influence occurred in many other varying ways. The extension workers CARE trained were young adults from the area, who would continue to live and work in the area after CARE withdrew. Yet, CARE deliberately chose to train women and men in equal numbers, which would not have occurred if selection had been left to the unequal gender norms of the community. CARE allowed local practices to form the focus of their research, but the CARE agroforesters also made observations and conducted trials to relate seedling survival, growth rates, nutrient contributions, and cash values of products of different species to the soils, planting densities, and pruning and harvesting practices, and so on. The results of these investigations informed the advice they gave to the local farmers and to agroforesters in other areas of the Sahelian region.

CARE's emphasis on achieving meaningful local participation stemmed from an awareness that a successful project would require a complex set of negotiations involving the organization funding the project and government bodies. Indeed, CARE deliberately located this project in an area without significant involvement by government forestry workers so that the project could become established and visibly successful before it incited bureaucratic interference. In retrospect, CARE officials concluded that if this project were to be taken as a model for other areas and if the extension networks they had established were to remain viable, they needed more government endorsement than they had sought. This reservation aside, the participatory approaches of subsequent CARE projects in agriculture, forestry, healthcare, and other areas drew heavily on the model of the Kenyan agroforestry project. The success of the agroforestry project was evident when, during the evaluation process, the farmers were asked: "Who decided which species to grow? Who owns the production process?" The answer to both questions was clear; the farmers exclaimed: "These trees are ours!"

Participation in rural development projects is not always invoked with the sincerity or the success evident in the CARE project. Indeed, the mandate for participation can be wielded in disempowering ways by State or International agencies (Agrawal 2001; Ribot 1999; see also Peters 1996 for a review of the politics of participation and participation rhetoric). Nevertheless, in industrialized countries as well as in poor rural regions environmental planning and management increasingly builds in stakeholder collaboration, that is, explicit procedures for participation of representatives of community groups, government agencies, corporations, and private property owners.

Of course, participation, collaboration, constituency-building, and Action Research are not confined to rural development and environmental issues. One notable organization that has been "facilitating a culture of participation" in community and institutional development around the world since the 1970s is the Institute of Cultural Affairs (ICA). To repeat the preamble from our description of the **Strategic *Personal* Planning** process, the basic propositions of the ICA workshop process include:

- Notwithstanding any initial impressions to the contrary, everyone has insight (wisdom) and we need everyone's insight for the wisest result.
- There is insight in every response. There are no wrong answers.
- We know more than we are, at first, prepared or able to acknowledge.
- When we are heard, we can better hear others and hear ourselves. This causes us to examine decisions made in advance about what the other people are like, what they are and are not capable of.
- The step-by-step workshop process thus aims to keep us listening actively to each other, foster mutual respect, and elicit more of our insight.
- Our initial conclusions may change, so we need to be open for surprises.
- What we come out with is very likely to be larger and more durable than what any one person came in with; the more so, the more voices that are brought out by the process.
- In particular, we will be engaged in carrying out and carrying on the plans we develop.
- In sum, the workshop process aims for the "greatest input, with greatest commitment and the least confusion, in the least time."

How these propositions translate into practice is illustrated in another excerpt from Taylor (2005, 207-210):

ICA's techniques have been developed through several decades of "facilitating a culture of participation" in community and institutional development. Their work anticipated and now exemplifies the post-Cold War emphasis on a vigorous civil society, that is, of institutions between the individual and, on one hand, the state and, on the other hand, the large corporation (Burbidge 1997). ICA planning workshops involve a neutral facilitator leading participants through four phases—practical vision, underlying obstacles, strategic directions, and action plans (Stanfield 2002). These mirror and make use of the "objective, reflective, interpretive, decisional" steps of shorter ICA **Focused Conversations**" (Stanfield 1997). The goal of ICA workshops is to elicit participation in a way that brings insights to the surface and ensures the full range of participants are invested in collaborating to bring the resulting plans or actions to fruition [see principles above and Stanfield 2002, especially his chart of old and new styles of social relations, p. xviii].

Such investment was evident, for example, after a community-wide planning process in the West Nipissing region of Ontario, 300 kilometers north of Toronto. In 1992, when the regional Economic Development Corporation (EDC) enlisted ICA to facilitate the process, industry closings had increased the traditionally high unemployment to crisis levels. As well as desiring specific plans, the EDC sought significant involvement of community residents. Twenty meetings with over 400 participants moved through the first three phases—vision, obstacles, and directions. The results were synthesized by a steering committee into common statements of the vision (see figure below), challenges, and strategic directions. A day-long workshop attended by 150 community residents was then held to identify specific projects and action plans, and to engage various groups in carrying out projects relevant to them.

Vision 20/20	**WEST NIPISSING VISION**							February 1993	
STRONG DIVERSIFIED ECONOMIC BASE			**EXCITING ATTRACTIVE COMMUNITY TO LIVE IN**			**ACTIVELY INVOLVED POPULATION**			
WIDELY PROMOTED TOURISM BASE	EXPANDED BUSINESS DEVELOPMENT	APPROPRIATE NATURAL RESOURCES DEVELOPMENT	WELL MAINTAINED EXPANDING INFRA-STRUCTURE	COMMUNITY BASED SERVICES	RESPONSIVE ACCOUNTABLE UNIFIED GOVERNMENT	ACTIVE INVOLVED COMMUNITY	IMPROVED RECREATION OPPORTUNITY	LIFELONG EDUCATION FACILITIES
Broad Based Tourism Promotion	Modern Recycling Facilities	Forestry Development	Improved Transportation Network Locally/Area	First Response Teams	Effective Cooperation Between Municipalities	Active Involvement of Citizens in All Community Developments	Youth Activities Promoted and Supported	Accessible Expanded Adult Education
Improved Four Season Accommodation	Northern Ontario Service Industry Centre	Expanded Local Agricultural Market		Community Based Services for Mental Health & Physically Challenged	Ongoing Citizen Involvement in Local Government	West Nipissing Team Cooperation	Improved Access to Lake Nipissing	
Accessible Waterways and Waterfronts	Appropriate Natural & Resource Based Industry		Well Serviced Community	Expanded Local Access to Specialized Clinics		West Nipissing Friendly Welcoming Community		Focused Job Training Programs
Packaged Tourist Attractions & Tours	Incentive Programs to Attract Businesses	Fish Hatcheries		Coordinated Integrated Services under One Roof	Local Service Boards in Unincorporated Municipalities	Rural Residential Development	Broadened Leisure Activities and Facilities	
Expanded Coordinated Community Festivals	Francophone Bilingual College	Clean Lake Nipissing	Environment-ally Responsive Community	Expanded Vibrant Senior Citizen Community	Re-evaluate Land Use By-laws	Open Communication across West Nipissing	Improved Organized Sports	Enhanced Post Secondary Education
	Local Businesses meet all needs			Restructured Social Assistance System		Youth Involved in Planning All Activities		
	Attract Government Offices							

The vision for West Nipissing region in Canada produced by a community-wide planning process in 1992 (from West Nipissing Economic Development Corporation 1993)

A follow-up evaluation five years later found that they could not simply check off plans that had been realized. The initial projects had spawned many others; indeed, the EDC had been able to shift from the role of initiating projects to that of supporting them. It made more sense, therefore, to assemble the accomplishments under the headings of the original vision and strategy documents. Over 150 specific developments were cited, which demonstrated a stronger and more diversified economic base, and a diminished dependence on provincial and national government social welfare programs. Equally importantly, the community now saw itself as responsible for these initiatives and developments, eclipsing the initial catalytic role of the EDC-ICA planning process. Still, the EDC appreciated the importance of that process and initiated a new round of facilitated community planning in 1999 (West Nipissing Economic Development Corporation 1993, 1999).

Another notable organization in the area of participation, collaboration, constituency-building is the Highlander Center, in Tennessee, which has "serve[d] as a catalyst for grassroots organizing and movement building in Appalachia and the South" since the 1930s. The words of Myles Horton (1905-1990)—at the start of this section and below—convey the philosophy that "answers to the problems facing society lie in the experiences of ordinary people" (HERC, n.d.), a philosophy that guides the popular education, participatory research, and cultural work that Highlander facilitates.

Myles Horton (in a 1983 interview with Bill Moyers) recounts his response to a priest who, frustrated at his own attempts to implement the Highlander approach in a labor school back in the early CIO days, tried to get at the problem by learning what books that had influenced Horton's life the most.

> "I can tell you, but it won't help you because like all people I got my own track of development; my own background is part of it.
> I grew up in a religious family. Undoubtedly the first book that influenced my life was the bible. No question about that..."
> [The priest] asked what particularly?
> "OK. There's the New Testament; there's the Old Testament. In the New Testament you learn about love. You can't be a revolutionary, you can't want to change society unless you love people—there's no point in it. OK, so you love people;

that's right out of the bible.

The other thing is the Old Testament tells us primarily about the creation. God was a creator. If people were born in God's image, you got to be creative; you can't be followers, puppets. You got to be creative."

RESOURCES

Included here are just a few entry points for you to explore the insights, experiences, and information from a wider world of research, writing, and engagement in change. (Full references are given in the References section.) More conventional texts that lay out the steps, decisions, and theories involved in research in your field can be readily found through an internet search of syllabi for research courses.

Updates and Supplements

Graduate courses based around the three frameworks:
Phases of Research and Engagement: syllabus, http://www.faculty.umb.edu/pjt/692.html; examples of student assignments, http://www.faculty.umb.edu/pjt/692Examples.html

Cycles and Epicycles of Action Research: syllabus, http://www.faculty.umb.edu/pjt/693.html; examples of student assignments, http://www.faculty.umb.edu/pjt/693examples.html

Creative Habits for Synthesis of Theory and Practice: syllabus, http://www.faculty.umb.edu/pjt/694.html

Online forums to engage the authors and others in conversation and sharing of resources, struggles, and accomplishments
General forum: http://cctnetwork.ning.com/forum/topics/taking-yourself-seriously-a

Support and coaching structure to get most participants to finish a project by a target date: http://cctnetwork.ning.com/forum/topics/support-and-coaching-structure-to-get-most-participants-to-finish

Probe-Create Change-Reflect blog, http://pcrcr.wordpress.com

Wiki version of book, with updated components, http://cct.wikispaces.umb.edu/TYS

Action Research

Calhoun, E. F. (1994). How to Use Action Research in the Self-Renewing School.

Craig, D. V. (2009). Action Research Essentials.

Highlander Research and Education Center, publications, http://www.highlandercenter.org/r-bookstore.asp

Horton, M. and B. Moyers (1983). "The adventures of a radical hillbilly: An interview with Myles Horton." (See also Video, Public Broadcasting System, 1981)

Schmuck, R. (1997 or 2006). Practical Action Research for Change.

See also the publications cited in Part 4 on Action Research and Participation.

Facilitation

Holman, P. and T. Devane, Eds. (1999). The Change Handbook: Group Methods for Shaping the Future.

Institute of Cultural Affairs, Canada, publications, http://icabookstore.mybigcommerce.com

Scharmer, O. (2009). Theory U: Leading from the Future as It Emerges.

Schuman, S., Ed. (2006). Creating a Culture of Collaboration: The International Association of Facilitators Handbook.

Senge, P., et al. (1994). The Fifth Discipline Fieldbook.

Stanfield, R. B., Ed. (1997). The Art of Focused Conversation.

Stanfield, R. B. (2002). The Workshop Book: From Individual Creativity to Group Action. (See useful excerpts on Google Books.)

Research

CCT Program (2010). Research and study competencies. http://www.cct.umb.edu/competencies.html (viewed 1 Dec 2011)

Denzin, N. K. and Y. S. Lincoln, Eds. (2005). The Sage Handbook of Qualitative Research.

Schloss, P. J. and M. A. Smith (1999). Conducting Research.

Writing

Boice, R. (1990). Professors as Writers: A Self-Help Guide to Productive Writing.

Daniel, D., et al. (2001). Take Charge of Your Writing: Discovering Writing Through Self-Assessment.

Elbow, P. (1981). Writing with Power.

Elbow, P. and P. Belanoff (2000). Summary of kinds of responses. Pp. 7ff in Sharing and Responding.

Turabian, K. L. (2007). A Manual For Writers of Term papers, Theses, and Dissertations.

References

Adams, F. with M. Horton (1975). Unearthing Seeds of Fire: The Idea of Highlander. Winston-Salem, NC: John F. Blair.

Agrawal, A. (2001). "State formation in community spaces?: The Forest Councils of Kumaon." Journal of Asian Studies 60(1): 1-32.

Boice, R. (1990). Professors as Writers: A Self-Help Guide to Productive Writing. Stillwater, OK: New Forums Press.

Borchers, J. and C. Maser (2001). Understanding Constraints in Sustainable Development. Chelsea, MI: Lewis.

Bradford, A. (1999). Guidelines for dialogue. http://www.cct.umb.edu/guidelinesdia.htm (viewed 2 Jan 2012)

Brown, P. (2007). Toxic Exposures: Contested Illnesses and the Environmental Health Movement. New York: Columbia University Press.

Burbidge, J., Ed. (1997). Beyond Prince and Merchant: Citizen Participation and the Rise of Civil Society. New York: Pact Publications.

Calhoun, E. F. (1994). How to Use Action Research in the Self-Renewing School. Alexandria, VA: ASCD.

Cameron, J. (2002). The Artist's Way. New York: Tarcher.

CCT (Critical and Creative Thinking Program) (2008). Overview. http://www.cct.umb.edu/overview.html (viewed 2 Sep 2008)

——— (2010). Research and study competencies. http://www.cct.umb.edu/competencies.html (viewed 1 Dec 2011)

Craig, D. V. (2009). Action Research Essentials. San Francisco: Jossey-Bass.

Critical Thinking Across The Curriculum Project (2011). Glossary. http://mcckc.edu/services/criticalthinking/criticalthinkingproject/glossary.asp (viewed 3 Dec 2011)

Daniel, D., C. Fauske, P. Galeno and D. Mael (2001). Take Charge of Your Writing: Discovering Writing Through Self-Assessment. Boston: Houghton Mifflin.

Denzin, N. K. and Y. S. Lincoln, Eds. (2005). The Sage Handbook of Qualitative Research. Thousand Oaks, CA: Sage.

Dervin, B. (1999) "Chaos, order, and sense-making: A proposed theory for information design." Pp. 35-57 in Jacobson, R. (ed.), Information Design. Cambridge, MA: MIT Press. http://communication.sbs.ohio-state.edu/sense-making/art/artabs dervin99mit.html (viewed 11 Jul 2011)

Doll, W. E. (1993). A Post-Modern Perspective on Curriculum. New York, Teachers College Press.

Elbow, P. (1981). Writing with Power. New York: Oxford University Press.

Elbow, P. and P. Belanoff (2000). "Summary of kinds of responses." Pp. 7ff in Sharing and Responding. Boston: McGraw-Hill.

Ennis, R. H. (1987). "A taxonomy of critical thinking dispositions and abilities." Pp. 9-26 in Baron, J. B. and R. J. Sternberg (eds.), Teaching Thinking Skills: Theory and Practice. New York, W. H. Freeman: 9-26.

Gibbs, L. M. (1982). Love Canal: My Story. Albany: State University of New York Press.

REFERENCES

Goode, E. (1998) "When bars say no the smoking," New York Times, 15 Dec.

Greenwald, N. (2000). "Learning from Problems." The Science Teacher 67(April): 28-32.

Greenwood, D. J. and M. Levin (1998). Introduction To Action Research: Social Research For Social Change. Thousand Oaks, CA: Sage.

Highlander Research and Education Center (n.d.), http://www.highlandercenter.org/about.asp (viewed 30 Nov 2011)

Holman, P. and T. Devane, Eds. (1999). The Change Handbook: Group Methods for Shaping the Future. San Francisco: Berrett-Koehler.

Horton, M. and B. Moyers (1983). "The adventures of a radical hillbilly: An interview with Myles Horton." Appalachian Journal 9(4): 248-285. (See also Video, Public Broadcasting System, 1981)

Institute of Cultural Affairs, http://ica-associates.ca/ (viewed 30 Nov 2011)

Isaacs, W. (1999). Dialogue and the Art of Thinking Together. New York: Currency.

Kemmis, S. and R. McTaggart (2005). "Participatory Action Research: Communicative Action and the Public Sphere." Pp. 559-603 in Denzin, N. and Y. S. Lincoln (eds.), The Sage Handbook of Qualitative Research. Thousand Oaks, CA: Sage.

Legendre, B. (n.d.). Exploring your writing preferences. Ithaca, N.Y.: Cornell University Writing Workshop (available at http://www.faculty.umb.edu/pjt/legendre.pdf; viewed 9 July 2010)

NewSSC (New England Workshop on Science and Social Change) (2008). Links to webpages and associated materials for workshops. http://www.stv.umb.edu/newssc.html (viewed 28 Aug 2008)

Palmer, P. J. (2000). Let Your Life Speak: Listening for the Voice of Vocation. San Francisco: Jossey-Bass.

Park, P., M. Brydon-Miller, B. Hall, T. Jackson (eds.) (1993). Voices of Change: Participatory Research in the United States and Canada. Westport, CT: Bergin & Garvey.

Peters, P. (1996). "Who's local here? The politics of participation in development." Cultural Survival Quarterly 20(3): 22-60.

Pietro, D. S. (ed.) (1983). Evaluation Sourcebook. New York: American Council of Voluntary Agencies for Foreign Service.

Ribot, J. C. (1999). "Decentralisation, participation and accountability in Sahelian forestry: Legal instruments of political-administrative control." Africa 69(1): 23-65.

Ross, R. (1994). "Ladder of Inference." Pp. 242-246 in Senge, P., A. Kleiner, C. Roberts, R. Ross, and B. Smith, The Fifth Discipline Fieldbook. New York: Currency.

Scharmer, O. (2009). Theory U: Leading from the Future as It Emerges. San Francisco: Berrett-Koehler Publishers.

Schloss, P. J. and M. A. Smith (1999). Conducting Research. Upper Saddle River: Prentice Hall.

Schmuck, R. (1997 or 2006). Practical Action Research for Change. Arlington Heights, IL: Skylight.

Schuman, S., Ed. (2006). Creating a Culture of Collaboration: The International Association of Facilitators Handbook. San Francisco, Jossey-Bass.

Selener, D. (1997). Participatory Action Research and Social Change. Ithaca, NY: Cornell University Press.

Senge, P., A. Kleiner, C. Roberts, R. Ross, B. Smith (1994). The Fifth Discipline Fieldbook. New York: Currency.

Stanfield, B. (Ed.) (1997). The Art of Focused Conversation. Toronto: Canadian Institute of Cultural Affairs.

———— (2002) The Workshop Book: From Individual Creativity to Group Action. Toronto: Canadian Institute of Cultural Affairs.

STEMTEC (1998) Workshop on science, technology, engineering and mathematics education, University of Massachusetts Medical School, November

Taylor, P. J. (1999). From 'dialogue around written work' to 'taking initiative'. http://www.faculty.umb.edu/pjt/citreport.html (viewed 28 Aug 2008)

———— (2001). Generating environmental knowledge and inquiry through workshop processes. http://www.faculty.umb.edu/pjt/ECOS.html (viewed 28 Aug 2008)

———— (2005). Unruly Complexity: Ecology, Interpretation, Engagement. Chicago, University of Chicago Press.

———— (2008). "Developing Critical Thinking is Like a Journey." In Ollington, G. F., Teachers and Teaching Strategies, Problems and Innovations. Hauppauge, NY, Nova Science Publishers.

———— (2009). Step-by-step presentation of the Cycles and Epicycles framework of Action Research. http://www.faculty.umb.edu/pjt/ARcycling2.html (viewed 28 Nov 2011)

————, S. J. Fifield, C. Young. (2011). "Cultivating Collaborators: Concepts and Questions Emerging Interactively From An Evolving, Interdisciplinary Workshop." Science as Culture, 21:89-105.

Thomashow, M. (1995) Ecological Identity: Becoming a Reflective Environmentalist. Cambridge, MA: MIT Press.

Tuecke, P. (2000). Creating a wall of wonder with the TOP environmental scan. International Association of Facilitators, Toronto, Canada, April 27 - 30.
http://www.faculty.umb.edu/pjt/tuecke00.pdf (viewed 6 Jul 2011)

Turabian, K. L. (2007). A Manual For Writers of Term papers, Theses, and Dissertations. Chicago, University of Chicago Press.

Vonk, R. (1987). "Indigenous agroforestry systems: A case study from the CARE-Kenya agroforestry extension program, part I & II." Papers delivered to the Social Forestry Program at the University of California, Berkeley, 21 & 22 September.

Weissglass, J. (1990). "Constructivist listening for empowerment and change." The Educational Forum 54(4): 351-370.

West Nipissing Economic Development Corporation (1993). Vision 20/20: Shaping our futures together, Executive Summary. (April 1993).

———— (1999). Vision 2000 Plus, Executive Summary. (June 1999).

Wiggins, G. P. and J. McTighe (2005). Understanding by Design. Alexandria, VA: Association for Supervision and Curriculum Development.

Williams, R. (1983). Keywords: A Vocabulary of Culture and Society. New York, Oxford University Press.

Comments on the *Taking Yourself Seriously* approach to developing as a researcher, writer and agent of change

a healthcare professional and story-teller
"I learned is to 'hold my ideas loosely', which means accepting my own idea as a valid one but always leaving space open to take in counterarguments."

"I learned to give myself permission to be circular and come back to previous steps or thoughts, and I actually became more comfortable doing so."

"I was able to get engaged in a project that I was able to actually use in work, which was extremely satisfying. The whole process encouraged me, and I felt very empowered as a change agent, which could be an exhilarating feeling."

a biologist-turned-web designer
"I really had not been used to thinking about my own thinking, so learning to do that also helped me to slow down and start to look away from the career path that I had been taking for granted."

"Many of my colleagues... went to school to become web developers but [this approach] allowed me to believe that traditional classes are not always necessary to learn. [The] teachings, which included networking, self-study, research, meta-cognition, and enjoying the process (in an organized way), kept me believing that I could learn what was necessary to succeed on my own."

a teacher
"Doing good research involves not just letting the information of others supersede your own, but thinking about your own understanding as lying at the top of past research, standing beyond it but also being supported by it."

"I found that my experience in the courses helped me to accept feedback from other professionals. I am more comfortable with listening to why my own ideas might not work or need further evaluation. This even happens to the point where I find reasons now to seek out this kind of feedback."

"I have become much more patient with people, recognizing more fully that people have their own timelines and that students need to have some freedom to say when they have had enough during a learning experience."

"I now consider reflection and sharing an important part of evolution of a person in their learning. Reflection means not only thinking about our own experiences and retrieving memories or feelings, but also then sharing reflections with others as a way of allowing the self to receive feedback. Doing this shows a sophistication as a learner."

an adult educator
"I took away the idea of putting one's action into a ritual, where the ritual is a way of helping oneself create some consistency in organizing the process of work and even developing habits of work that have a sacred quality."

"I had viewed research as a process of collecting information into a sort of database and reviewing it effectively. I have now revised my notions to include a more broad understanding of interconnectedness between people and ideas. An important part of research is to keep relationships going."

"I liked the way that [I learned] to play with confusion and to consider this in my own teaching. I have come to see confusion mostly as an indication that people are uncomfortable with freedom and want to get comfortable by knowing what is expected."

"[The approach has] had a profound effect on my professional development as an educator. The "system"... for getting graduate students to "take themselves seriously" cultivates graduate students' ability to work through big projects of diverse forms. The methods I learned from [this] approach have been a tremendous benefit to me as a writer, educator, presenter, and in organizing my personal projects as well."

a teacher, currently working in publishing
"One of the most useful idea from the courses was the use of dialogue, which helps to slow down the procedures used by the company. There's a tension between management's need to make quick decisions and desire to have real dialogue around proposed changes—changes to the internal company operational procedures as well as to evaluating the quality of what the company is doing with its publications."

"[This approach has] instilled in me a sense of responsibility and empowerment to be an agent of change for the betterment of my professional and personal communities."

a college librarian
"I was asked to pay attention to what I actually could do instead of what I could not. This enabled me to (1) step back and let go of a huge technical problem (that I really had no ability or interest to solve), and (2) identify where my actual interest rested and actual skills intersected with what needed to be done. I realized that I could unite my passion to advance visual thinking with my skills in communication and group facilitation."

Taking Yourself Seriously

A field-book of tools and processes to help readers in all fields develop as researchers, writers, and agents of change

A wide range of tools and processes for research, writing, and collaboration are defined and described—from Governing Question to GOSP, Plus-Delta feedback to Process Review, and Supportive Listening to Sense of Place Map. The tools and processes are linked to three frameworks that lend themselves to adaptation by teachers and other advisors:
- A set of ten Phases of Research and Engagement, which researchers move through and later revisit in light of other people's responses to work in progress and what is learned using tools from the other phases;
- Cycles and Epicycles of Action Research, which emphasizes reflection and dialogue to shape ideas about what action is needed and how to build a constituency to implement the change; and
- Creative Habits for Synthesis of theory and practice.

Researchers and writers working under these frameworks participate in Dialogue around Written Work and in Making Space for Taking Initiative In and Through Relationships. These processes help researchers and writers align their questions and ideas, aspirations, ability to take or influence action, and relationships with other people. Bringing those dimensions of research and engagement into alignment is the crux of *taking yourself seriously*. The tools, processes, and frameworks are illustrated through excerpts from two projects: one engaging adult learning communities in using the principles of theater arts to prepare them to create social change; the other involving collaborative play among teachers in curriculum planning. A final section provides entry points for students and educators to explore insights, experiences, and information from a wider world of research, writing, and engagement in change.

Peter Taylor is a Professor at the University of Massachusetts Boston where he directs the Graduate Program in Critical and Creative Thinking and the undergraduate Program on Science, Technology and Values. His research and writing links innovation in teaching and interdisciplinary collaboration with studies of the complexity of environmental and health sciences in their social context. This combination is evident in his 2005 book, *Unruly Complexity: Ecology, Interpretation, Engagement* (University of Chicago Press).

Jeremy Szteiter is a 2009 graduate of the Critical and Creative Thinking program and now serves as the Program's Assistant Coordinator. His work has centered around community-based and adult education and has involved managing, developing, and teaching programs to lifelong learners, with an emphasis on a learning process that involves the teaching of others what has been learned and supporting the growth of individuals to become teachers of what they know.

CPSIA information can be obtained at www.ICGtesting.com
Printed in the USA
LVOW05s1736280115

424741LV00019B/805/P